FIRST FOLIO

FIRST FOLIO

A Little Book of Folio Forewords

Introduced by Catherine Taylor

The Folio Society
London 2008

CONTENTS

CONTENTS

ILLUSTRATIONS

INTRODUCTION

In this collection, fifteen of today's finest writers introduce books which hold enormous significance for them – and although some of the choices might at first seem surprising, all are eminently fitting. The themes are eternal – war, power, love, childhood, nostalgia, heroes and anti-heroes, the influence of travel and experience of differing cultures, the circumlocutions of the human brain and the arguably greater complexities of the human heart.

'Between the more or less, of course, is where fiction usually happens,' writes John Sutherland on one of the most powerful indictments of war ever produced – Kurt Vonnegut's *Slaughterhouse-Five*. Vonnegut drew on his own eyewitness experiences of the decimation of Dresden, commenting later that 'all organic things were consumed' in the 1945 mass bombing of the German city. As Sutherland points out, *Slaughterhouse-Five* is 'like a fly trapped in a blob of amber . . . it is very much a novel of its time, the 1960s'. But what a novel.

Just over seventy years before Vonnegut, H. G. Wells was inventing a new genre of writing – science fiction. In perhaps his most famous work, *The War of the Worlds*, Wells's late nineteenth-century depiction of a tranquil Surrey at the mercy of an alien invasion – with Wells its lower middle-class hero – seems eerily prescient of twenty-first-century Britain. According to Iain Sinclair, *The War of the Worlds* also 'anticipates the hopelessness of coming ecological disaster, rivers choked with red weed'; a time when society understands that 'terror is a given, part of the human contract', and in so doing, the book 'makes the journey from sensationalist incident to moral parable'.

A sixteenth-century political theorist who turned his own disgraced exile to his advantage and formulated a timeless treatise on statecraft, in which an Italian saviour repels foreign usurpers – look no further than Niccoló Machiavelli. And his relevance to our own period of history? As Tim Parks so cogently puts it: 'After the obvious parallels have sprung to mind, and we have marvelled at how applicable the Renaissance writer's precepts still are, the further surprise is our growing awareness that, like it or not, the way we judge the wars of our times is indeed "Machiavellian".'

From war to love, and another famous Italian exile. In Frances Wilson's vivid introduction to Casanova's memoirs she explains that 'the role in which he excelled, and the one which demanded his most brilliant performances, was that of the confidence trickster'. Sifting through the evidence, she asks, was the great seducer mainly the seduced? From a life of supposed rakishness, eventually poverty and rejection forced him, at the age of fifty-seven, to accept the position of librarian at Dux Castle in Bohemia, where he was to spend the remaining thirteen years of his life composing his tantalising memoirs.

Another eighteenth-century rake – this time fictional – is Jonathan Coe's choice. 'When people talk of *Tom Jones*, they like to use words such as "bawdy" and "lusty",' shudders Coe. 'I have even seen the novel described, without irony or apology, as "lad-lit".' Yet he argues that we should look beyond 'the whiff of embarrassment' and concentrate on Henry Fielding 'the novelist, and recognise him as the bold and sophisticated pioneer that he was'.

For Tolstoy, the profound spiritual and religious crisis of his later life made him believe that, 'In deriding *Anna Karenina*, he might distract attention from this exposure of his earlier self', a self which conveyed 'the harm that will be done throughout the novel by deception and broken faith'. Helen Dunmore writes that *Anna Karenina* deals with so much more than the tale of a married woman falling in love with an officer. 'Adultery represents the breaking of a contract not only between two individuals but between society and individual sexual desires.'

There is no more sympathetic and elliptical observer of society's norms than Henry James. In *The Golden Bowl*, two lovers are disposed to continue their relationship even after they marry, respectively, a father and his daughter. For Colm Tóibín, author of *The Master*, the Man Booker-shortlisted homage to James, *The Golden Bowl* represents 'James's last important work of fiction', yet in his essay on the genesis of the novel, Tóibín reveals how the seeds of James's masterpiece of late style exist in many of his earlier short stories, and is even foreshadowed by *The Portrait of a Lady*.

Ford Madox Ford's short novel, *The Good Soldier*, with its repressed characters, startling plot and brilliant use of language, certainly bears many Jamesian hallmarks. Julian Barnes, in his preface, reminds us that Ford's dramatic – some might say melodramatic – life, 'deeply complicated and overlapping, and made worse for all concerned by his indecisiveness, self-indulgence and economy with the truth', was heavily reflected in his fiction. Barnes warns the reader: 'We must prowl soft-footed through this text, alive for every board's moan and plaint.'

In her piece on *The Pink Fairy Book*, A. S. Byatt, herself a consummate weaver of tales, discloses that as a child she was simultaneously horrified and fascinated by the great nineteenth-century folklorist Andrew Lang's collections of fairytales – in this volume an international emporium originating from Africa and Japan as well as Europe and especially Denmark, where Hans Christian Andersen turns fairy into something approaching horror. As Byatt notes: 'One of my earliest discoveries, that went to making me a writer, was that Hans Andersen was an author, with his own purposes and intents, one of which – I was deeply shocked – was to make me, the reader, disturbed and unhappy.'

Childhood is much less magically evoked in Charles Dickens's intensely autobiographical *Oliver Twist* in which, Dickens's biographer Peter Ackroyd explains, 'some of the salient facts of Dickens's childhood misery are carried over into the fictional narrative'. In fact, 'It has often been said that this was the first novel that has a child as its central character. That is true enough, but it is also significant as the first novel in which a suffering child – a victim of the public world – is made audible and visible to a large general audience of readers.'

Richard Holmes, whose first foray into biography, *Footsteps*, famously recreates Robert Louis Stevenson's *Travels with a Donkey in the Cevennes*, languorously opens his essay on Stevenson thus: 'I was eighteen years old and lying on Mount Lozère, high up in the remote Cévennes, when I first read Stevenson's heady paean to travel and travel writing. I was burning with sun and wind and loneliness, but had just found a spring, bubbling up out of the stony turf. I drank the ice-cold water, and read Stevenson's words in deep, alternating gulps.' Stevenson the life-affirmer, the insouciant, the reporter, leaps from the page.

It's an interesting point that one of Ireland's best-loved books was written by someone born in India to Scottish parents. To Fergal Keane, who makes it, this fact is irrelevant – David Thomson's *Woodbrook* is 'part love story, social history, coming-of-age narrative and elegy.

Above all it is a profound meditation on the experience of loss.' For a foreign correspondent like Keane, Thomson's account of his time as a tutor to an Anglo-Irish family in County Sligo between the wars is a book which frequently accompanies him far from home. 'With *Woodbrook* I can smell the damp hills, even in the Iraqi desert.'

Still regarded as Ireland's finest poet, Sligo native W. B. Yeats is traced in Roy Foster's introduction from his early Romantic bohemianism as extoller of the Celtic Twilight to questing spiritualist and then nationalist once again in the Irish Free State. According to Foster, Yeats was motivated by a 'determination to exoticise Irishness, to proclaim the essential difference and originality of his country's culture. This may reflect his own uncertain status – Protestant, slightly *déclassé*, living between London, Dublin and Sligo at the whim of his splendidly Bohemian father.'

The quintessentially English Anthony Powell wrote of his hugely popular twelve-book series *A Dance to the Music of Time* that 'autobiographical material produced by a professional novelist is bound to raise speculation as to how much direct experience has found a place in his fiction'. And Powell certainly drew on his contemporaries to create, as William Trevor reasons, 'a social comedy that eschews the conventional complexities of plot that so successfully energised the great novels of the Victorians'.

Powell's 'shadowing of the real by the imaginary' leads to his main protagonist Nicholas Jenkins cultivating an interest in Robert Burton's *The Anatomy of Melancholy* – coincidentally Philip Pullman's literature of choice. If *A Dance to the Music of Time* is long, Burton's disquisition on the origins of melancholy and its various antidotes just about exceeds it. Yet Pullman feels that this seventeenth-century curiosity is far from lugubrious, rather 'the revelation of a personality, and that personality is so vivid and generous, so humorous, so humane, so tolerant and cranky and wise, so filled with bizarre knowledge and so rich in absurd and touching anecdotes, that an hour in his company is a stimulant to the soul'. As it is hoped these varied, stimulating essays will prove to be.

CATHERINE TAYLOR
FICTION & LITERATURE PUBLISHER
THE FOLIO SOCIETY

FIRST FOLIO

Tim Parks on

THE PRINCE,

by Niccolò Machiavelli

He is still a scandal. Yet to read Machiavelli is also and always to take a very deep breath of fresh air, and that despite the almost five hundred years that have elapsed since he wrote *The Prince*. How can these conflicting reactions coincide? The fresh and bracing air blows, no doubt, from our immediate sense that this man is telling the truth about realities normally sugared over with rhetoric. The scandal lies in the fact that Machiavelli himself is not scandalised by the bitter truth he tells.

The very idea behind *The Prince* overturns any official hierarchy of values, whether ancient or modern. Machiavelli decides to give us a manual not of how a prince, or political leader, *should* behave, but how he *must* behave *if he wishes to hold on to power*. Every action will be judged in the light of that one goal. Power thus becomes, at least for the prince, an absolute value. There is no talk of a man's soul. There is no question of power being sought in order to carry out some benevolent programme of reform. The good of the people is not an issue, or even a side issue. The prince must hold on to power . . . *è basta*.

Societies and military strategies, individual and collective psychologies are rapidly and efficiently analysed. A wide variety of possible circumstances are established and enquired into. Examples are given from classical literature and recent history. The aim is never to savour the *achievements* of a given culture, to assess the attractions or otherwise of this or that political system, the balance of weal and woe under this or that regime: what we need to know is how, in each specific situation, a prince can best consolidate his authority and security. The underlying assumption is that, whatever may have

3

been written in the past, political leaders have always put power first and foremost, and indeed that any other form of behaviour would be folly.

The scandal of the book is not felt in its famous general statements: that the end justifies the means; that nothing is so self-defeating as generosity; that men must be pampered or crushed; that there is no surer way of keeping possession of a territory than by devastation, etc. It is easy to imagine these formulations arising from the transgressive glee of the talented writer who simply enjoys turning the world upside down.

No, it is when Machiavelli gives concrete examples and then moves on rapidly without comment that we begin to gasp: the Venetians find that their mercenary leader Carmagnola is not really fighting hard any more, but they are afraid that if they dismiss him he will walk off with some of the territory he had previously captured for them: 'So, for safety's sake, they were forced to kill him.' Hiero of Syracuse, when given command of his country's army, 'realised that the mercenaries were useless . . . It seemed to him impossible either to keep them or to disband them, so he had them all cut to pieces.' Cesare Borgia, having tamed and unified the Romagna with the help of the cruel minister Remirro De Orco, decides to deflect the hatred of the people from himself by putting the blame on the minister and then doing away with him: 'One morning, Remirro's body was found cut in two pieces on the piazza at Cesena, with a block of wood and a bloody knife beside it. The brutality of this spectacle kept the people of the Romagna for a time appeased and stupefied.' Borgia then consolidates his position by 'destroying all the families of the rulers he had despoiled'. 'I cannot possibly censure him,' Machiavelli concludes, because 'he could not have conducted himself other than the way he did.'

This sense of coercion, of there being simply no alternative to brutal and murderous behaviour, is central to Machiavelli's at once pessimistic yet strangely gung-ho vision. It involves the admission that there is a profound mismatch between the qualities that we actually appreciate in a person – generosity, loyalty, compassion, modesty – and the qualities that bring political success – calculation and ruthlessness. As Machiavelli sees it, this mismatch occurs because people in general are greedy, short-sighted and impressionable, and must be treated accordingly if a leader is to survive. 'I know everyone will agree', he concedes, 'that it would be most laudable if a prince possessed all the qualities deemed to be good among those I have enumerated. But, because of conditions in the world, princes cannot have those qualities . . .'

Since the modern English reader of Machiavelli has largely been brought up on a rationalist, utilitarian philosophy which ties itself in knots to demonstrate that, given the right kind of government, self-interest, collective interest *and* Christian values can all be reconciled, it is something of a relief to come across a writer who wastes no time with such utopian nonsense. Yet though Machiavelli never actually welcomes the world's awfulness and certainly never rejoices in cruelty, our own upbringing is such that we cannot help but feel that he might at least have *seemed* to be a little shocked by it all.

Seeming is an important issue in *The Prince*. Given that moral qualities are no longer to be taken as guides for correct behaviour, what, then, is their importance? They become no more than attractions. It is *attractive* when a man is compassionate, generous and modest. It is attractive when a man keeps his word and shows loyalty to friends. We are in the realm of aesthetics, not moral imperatives. And what is attractive, of course, can be manipulated as a tool of persuasion. So even if a prince is actually better off without certain moral qualities, he should *appear* to have them, because people will be impressed. In particular, he should appear to be devout in his religious beliefs. 'The common people are always impressed by appearances and results,' Machiavelli tells us. But he leaves us in no doubt that, if you have to choose between the two, the crucial factor is the result.

One of the great pleasures of reading and rereading *The Prince* is the way it prompts us to assess contemporary politicians and the wars of our own time in the light of Machiavelli's precepts and examples. To read *The Prince* in the 1980s was, inevitably, to have Thatcher and Reagan very much on one's mind, to think about American interference in Nicaragua or the British adventure in the Falklands as Machiavelli might have thought of them. Returning to the book in 2006, a reader is inevitably struck by how many of his observations could be applied directly to the Anglo-American invasion of Iraq of 2005, or indeed to many other such enterprises. This passage, for example, would seem applicable to any post-invasion situation:

A prince is always compelled to injure those who have made him the new ruler, subjecting them to the troops and imposing the endless other hardships which his new conquest entails. As a result, you are opposed by all those you have injured . . . and you cannot keep the friendship of those who have put you there; you cannot satisfy them in the way they had taken for granted, yet you cannot use strong medicine on them, as you are in their debt. For always, no matter how powerful one's armies, to enter a country one needs the goodwill of the inhabitants.

Future readers, no doubt, will have other wars to think about as they turn the pages of *The Prince*. That fact alone is a sad confirmation of Machiavelli's understanding of international politics. Yet after the obvious parallels have sprung to mind, and we have marvelled at how applicable the Renaissance writer's precepts still are, the further surprise is our growing awareness that, like it or not, the way we judge the wars of our times is indeed 'Machiavellian'. Would we be so critical of Suez, of Vietnam, of Iraq, if these adventures had succeeded? Wouldn't we rather begin to think of them as we think about Korea, or the Falklands? We do not, that is, judge the action in and for itself on a moral basis, but in terms of the consequences it produces. Which is the same as saying that for us, as for Machiavelli, the end justifies the means.

'The wish to acquire more', *The Prince* laconically reminds us, 'is admittedly a very natural and common thing; and when men succeed in this they are always praised rather than condemned. But when they lack the ability to do so and yet want to acquire more at all costs, they deserve condemnation for their mistakes.' If there is a difference between ourselves and the Florentine writer in this regard, it is that he remembers to condemn the adventurers for their *mistakes*, while most of us prefer the comfort of a moral high ground, imagining we would have condemned the adventure even had it been successful.

Are we, then, simply to accept Machiavelli lock, stock and barrel? In many ways he presents us with the same problem as the lesser-known but even more disturbing Max Stirner, who in *The Ego and His Own* extended the amoral Machiavellian power struggle to the life of every individual, rejecting the notion that there could be any moral limitation on anyone's behaviour: for Stirner, the only question a person must ask before doing what he wants or taking what he desires is: do I have the power to get away with this or not?

Certainly it would be foolish not to be warned by what Machiavelli has to tell us about politicians and politics in general. We must thank him for his clear-sightedness. Yet a charming ingenuity in *The Prince* allows us at least to imagine a response to what appears to be a closed and largely depressing system of thought. Why did Machiavelli publish the book?

Ostensibly written in the attempt to have Lorenzo de' Medici give him some position in Florentine government, *The Prince* is obviously self-defeating. Who would ever employ as his minister a man who has gone on record as presenting politics as a matter of pure power? If Machiavelli himself remarked that leaders gain from appearing to cultivate a refined moral sense and strong religious beliefs, why did he not at least hint at these qualities himself, or find some moral camouflage for his work, or put the book in Lorenzo's hands for private consultation only?

The answer has to be that as he was writing, Machiavelli allowed himself to be seduced by the desire to tell the truth come what may, a principle which thus for him, in this text at least, takes on a higher value than the mere quest for power. And in exposing the amoral nature of politics he actually and rather ironically threatens the way the political game is played. If it has not been possible, for example, for our contemporary armed forces in the West simply to lay waste to the various countries they have recently invaded, that may, in some tiny measure, be due to the kind of awareness that Machiavelli stimulated with this book, not in princes, perhaps, but certainly in their subjects.

Richard Holmes on

TRAVELS WITH
ROBERT LOUIS STEVENSON,

by R. L. Stevenson

I was eighteen years old and lying on Mont Lozère, high up in the remote Cévennes, when I first read Stevenson's heady paean to travel and travel writing. I was burning with sun and wind and loneliness, but had just found a spring, bubbling up out of the stony turf. I drank the ice-cold water, and read Stevenson's words, in deep, alternating gulps. Both made me wonderfully giddy. They sharpened rather than slaked my thirst.

> For my part I travel not to go anywhere, but to go; I travel for travel's sake. And to write about it afterwards, if only the public will be so condescending as to read. The great affair is to move; to feel the needs and hitches of life a little more nearly, to get down off this feather bed of civilisation, and to find the globe granite underfoot and strewn with cutting flints.
>
> [*Cevennes Journal*]

This is obviously a young man's declaration (Stevenson was twenty-seven), and written for other young men too. But, less obviously, it is also the angry declaration of an invalid against his fate. The tone and quality of this defiance make Stevenson's travel writing unique and enduring. And also magically uplifting to read – and re-read.

Born in Victorian Edinburgh in 1850, Stevenson undertook his earliest journeys quite literally from a feather bed, though it was a lonely and often frightening one – an only child's sickbed. As a fra-

8

gile, coughing, often feverish little boy, marooned beneath the bed-clothes and besieged by nightmares, he escaped as often as he could into 'the pleasant Land of Counterpane'.

Here he founded vast empires, navigated down mighty rivers, and crossed fantastic oceans. In the poem 'Travel', written years later from another, adult sickbed in Hyères, France, he recalled these childish longings with perfect fidelity:

> I should like to rise and go
> Where the golden apples grow;
> Where below another sky
> Parrot islands anchored lie,
> And, watched by cockatoos and goats,
> Lonely Crusoes building boats . . .
> [*A Child's Garden of Verses*]

Unlike most of us, Stevenson remained wonderfully faithful to his childhood dreams. Fidelity, like stoic courage, was intrinsic to his character. All his life he fought chronic illness with chronic adventure. The incurable invalid (whose tubercular lungs haemor-rhaged with terrifying regularity) became one of the most intrepid and inveterate travellers of his generation.

Teenage rambles over the Pentland Hills, and sailing trips round the wild shores of the Scottish Highlands, led southwards in his twenties to Belgium, France, Italy and Switzerland. His first published essay, written when he was twenty-three, was en-titled 'Roads'. He wrote: '*Sehnsucht* – the passion for what is ever beyond – is livingly expressed in that white riband of possible travel . . .'

The harsher counterpoint between illness and escape is haunt-ingly explored in another early essay, 'Ordered South'. Here he wrote movingly of the 'imprisoned life' of the conventional Vic-torian invalid that sometimes threatened to overwhelm him.

The world is disenchanted for him. He seems to himself to touch things with muffled hands, and to see them through a veil . . . Many a white town that sits far out on the promontory, many a

9

comely fold of wood on the mountain-side, beckons and allures his imagination day after day, and is yet as inaccessible to his feet as the clefts and gorges of the clouds.

Later his search for love, for family happiness, and always for health, led him to increasingly remote and exotic locations: to pioneering California (to find his future wife, Fanny Osbourne), to the wild Adirondack Mountains, to Australia, and – finally – to those 'parrot islands' of the South Pacific. When he died at the painfully early age of forty-four (from a brain haemorrhage rather than a tubercular one), the Land of Counterpane had been transformed into Stevenson's estate of Vailima, on Samoa. Nor was he lying in bed. He was standing on his own balcony, after a full day's writing, watching the beautiful Pacific dusk come down, and opening a bottle of his favourite old burgundy.

The extraordinary story of these lifelong wanderings is reflected in this remarkable three-volume set of Stevenson's miscellaneous travel writings. Covering some twenty years of work, they are hugely varied in length, tone and location. They include individual books, separate short essays, and a number of longer serialised articles written for English and American magazines (notably the pieces about Barbizon and the Lake District). The story is not continuous. Some well-known classics – notably *Travels with a Donkey*, which Folio has published elsewhere – are omitted. But rarer ones – the diverting first book, *An Inland Voyage*, and the haunting late work *In the South Seas* – fill out Stevenson's career of travel very well.

Volume One concerns Europe; Volume Two moves across to America (with some earlier material); and finally Volume Three takes us into the South Pacific. These divisions also reflect the three formative periods in Stevenson's life: first, the years of dandyish adventuring, up to the age of twenty-eight; then the search to establish his marriage with Fanny Osbourne; and, finally, from the age of thirty-seven, the great sea voyages and the quest for a settled home in exile.

Stevenson's whole biography could be set down in the form of a dotted line across the map, and eventually round much of the globe. He often spoke of the 'little pictorial maps' he held in his head of each of his journeys, and how many of his books began as imaginary expeditions through a landscape. In an essay on Walt Whitman he once remarked that 'there is a sense, of course, in which all true books are books of travel'. And his account of the conception of *Treasure Island* famously begins with the drawing of a map for his stepson, Lloyd. His wife Fanny Osbourne later remembered:

> To the end of his life he found the keenest pleasure in the study of a map, especially one of roads. Like Branwell Brontë, of whom he could never speak without emotion, he would sit poring over maps, making imaginary journeys . . . he knew the hours when railway

trains of London and Paris started, and when outgoing passenger ships left English and French ports.

Unlike many Victorian travel writers, Stevenson does much more than give a record of things seen and the strangeness of 'local colour'. Nothing could be further from a Bradshaw, a Baedeker or a Murray guide. Nor does he have much in common with the epic travel writers of the British Empire: Charles Doughty, Alexander Kinglake, Isabella Bird or Mary Kingsley. His writing is always extraordinarily intimate. It is picturesque, but intensely personal. It is a conscious exercise in style, but also a continuous self-portrait. He once wrote, 'a voyage is a piece of autobiography at best'.

It was in his travel writing, not his novels, that Stevenson created the confidential persona of 'R.L.S.' His fiction, for all its pace and colour, is a curiously impersonal machine, with its strong 'carpentering', its well-oiled suspense mechanisms, and its dependence on a powerful historical tradition of adventure writing: Daniel Defoe, Walter Scott, Alexandre Dumas and later maybe Émile Zola.

But his non-fiction influences are different ones, and perhaps less expected. He admired, imitated and learned from Samuel Pepys, James Boswell, Charles Lamb and William Hazlitt. He practised their styles – 'playing the sedulous ape' – and wrote critical appreciations of their work. He praised Pepys's 'unflinching sincerity' (remarking that we all would like to write 'such a diary in airy characters upon our brain'), and intended to write a biography of Hazlitt – 'the great master' of intimate Romantic prose. Hazlitt's 'On Going a Journey' is the basis for his own essay 'Walking Tours'.

Each of these admired writers is master of a recognisable, intimate, autobiographical voice. They are the deliberate 'personalities' of our literature: vivid, eccentric, confidential. Stevenson set out to create his own travel voice and persona: stoic and sincere, but also teasing, enchanting, flippant and seductive. The traveller becomes a storyteller who is always tempting us over the hills and far away: R.L.S. as the Pied Piper.

One of the revelations of these volumes is how much – and how fast – 'R.L.S.' altered and matured. The deliberate charmer, the *fumiste* and decorative-phrase maker of Volume One has been transformed into an impassioned advocate, realist and unflinching reporter by Volume Three. The man who described the bearded bohemian painters of Barbizon of 1875 seems totally different from the one who visited the lepers of Kona in 1889.

An Inland Voyage, published in 1878, was R.L.S.'s first book and the first time he deliberately set out to turn a private travel diary into popular literature. It was based on a canoe trip made with his aristocratic friend Walter Simpson in September 1876. Canoeing had become a fashionable sport, and R.L.S. had canoed regularly on the Firth of Forth with his 'mad' cousin Bob Stevenson and Simpson. *An Inland Voyage* was partly inspired by this vogue, and also by J. L. Molloy's successful account of a similar cruise down the Seine and into the Loire, *Our Autumn Holiday on French Rivers* (1874).

Stevenson's original, modest idea was to navigate from Belgium all the way to the Mediterranean. What he actually achieved, mostly in driving rain, was a desultory trip from Antwerp to Pontoise, just north of Paris – a distance of some two hundred miles covered in some three weeks. They sailed or paddled south-westwards through a network of canals and locks, and then into France down the river Oise.

They took two wooden ten-foot canoes with sails, the *Cigarette* (made of English oak) and the *Arethusa* (made of French cedar). The basic humorous device of the book is that the two travellers are given the names, and characters, of their boats. So Simpson is *Cigarette*, a solid, philosophic, totally reliable and very English presence, largely uncomplaining but often rather silent. While R.L.S. is *Arethusa*, voluble, flighty, inventive, generally unsafe on the water, rather pro-French and foolish, but a good deal of fun.

There is a wonderful sense in which nothing at all happens throughout the entire book: 'it was nothing but clay banks and willows, and rain'. They paddle along, get wet and cold each day, and then warm and dry and mildly drunk each night. Admittedly R.L.S. nearly drowns at one point, knocked out of his boat by a fallen tree; and Simpson nearly loses his temper at another, when insulted by a French landlady. Yet the book is brought alive by its style. Out of tiny haphazard incidents, R.L.S. spins a brilliant series of improvised essays on such things as church bells, balloons, wine, pedlars, patriotic songs, French logic, canal barges or cathedrals. They are sententious, but also highly observant. In a melancholy riverside inn he notices an empty birdcage with a slight bend in the bars where a lump of sugar used to be pushed, an emblem of lost care and love.

These mini-essays are presented as pure, dexterous improvisations, casually thrown off and allowed to spin and glitter in the light. Like a street juggler, Stevenson shows off his literary wares: his elaborations, digressions, inversions, exclamations, apothegms, asides. All is written in the fast, precocious, highly decorative, 'tuppenny-coloured' style of the early R.L.S.

> We lunched on a meadow inside a parallelogram of poplars. The leaves danced and prattled in the wind all round about us. The river hurried on meanwhile, and seemed to chide at our delay. Little we cared. The river knew where it was going; not so we . . . At that hour stockbrokers were shouting in the Paris Bourse for two or three per cent.; but we minded them as little as the sliding stream, and sacrificed a hecatomb of minutes to the gods of tobacco and digestion. Hurry is the resource of the faithless. Where a man can trust his own heart, and those of his friends, to-morrow is as good as to-day. And if he die in the meanwhile, why, then, there he dies, and the question is solved.

Naturally, R.L.S. develops a philosophy of canoeing. The beauty of his watery surroundings, the rhythmic simplicity of paddling, the detachment from the world of business and cities, is both physically and mentally healing. Travel becomes therapy, and even spiritual revelation.

> I was about as near Nirvana as would be convenient in practical life; and if this be so, I make the Buddhists my sincere compliments . . . A pity to go to the expense of laudanum, where here is a better paradise for nothing!
>
> This frame of mind was the great exploit of our voyage . . . It was the farthest piece of travel accomplished.

R.L.S.'s dandyism includes a continuous, flirtatious interest in women. Typical are the three girls he archly christens the Graces in the episode in Origny Sainte-Benoîte. The girls admire their canoes, suggestively stroking their wooden sides, and amorously comparing them to violins. *Arethusa* gallantly remarks that they are more usually compared to coffins. Later these maidens modestly turn their backs on the travellers, in the village street at dusk. But the next day they make a memorable farewell, chasing after the canoes along the river bank.

> . . . the foremost of the three leaped upon a tree-stump and kissed her hand to the canoeists. Not Diana herself, although this was more of a Venus after all, could have done a graceful thing more gracefully. 'Come back again!' she cried; and all the others echoed her; and the hills about Origny repeated the words, 'Come back.'

Self-mockery is also part of the R.L.S. persona. Their glorious reception by a democratic Belgian boating club, ironically named the Royal Sport Nautique, is painfully compared with that of the humiliating rejection by the landlady of the snobby inn at 'La Fère of Cursed Memory', who bundles them out into the street.

This mockery deepens to a more subtle and pervasive sense that the travellers are suspect and déclassé. They are frequently mistaken for pedlars, carrying their faintly sinister 'india-rubber bags' into each village at dusk. They are stared at suspiciously in villages, turned away from inns, followed by crowds of small children who sometimes spit at them from the bridges. (Here R.L.S. remarks genially that these small boys have acted 'with a true conservative feeling'.)

Yet the subversive idea that the traveller sees the true underside of society and the real conditions of poverty and rejection was soon to become a major theme of Stevenson's writing. 'As long as you keep in the upper regions, with all the world bowing to you as you go, social arrangements have a very handsome air; but once get under the wheels, and you wish society were at the devil.'

The Epilogue adds an incident where R.L.S. is actually arrested as a vagabond or a spy. He is only released when Simpson –

identified as the son of a Scottish baronet on his passport – comes to vouch for him. Here the whimsy has gained a distinct, satirical edge.

It also touches unexpectedly on a larger, grimmer moment of history. Their whole journey is shadowed by the memories of the recent Franco-Prussian War (1870–1) and the national shame of France's defeat. The French towns often hold military garrisons, and there are troop manoeuvres, reveille trumpets, and the firing of distant guns. They encounter drunken, prickly militia in the inns. The nervousness they excite in the small riverside villages, and the noisy chauvinism in the larger towns, is set uneasily against their own holiday nonchalance.

For the modern reader this also holds a tragic prophecy. The bucolic route of the canoeists traverses the flat frontier countryside where many of the most murderous battles of the Great War were fought a generation later. In 1918 the English poet Wilfred Owen was killed on exactly this section of the Sambre–Oise Canal.

Nevertheless, at the time the little book may be said to have launched a whole flotilla of innocent, Arcadian, riverside adventures. Not least of these were Jerome K. Jerome's *Three Men in a Boat* (1889) and Kenneth Grahame's *Wind in the Willows* (1908).

Stevenson's Arcadian attitude had hardened greatly by the time he wrote *Across the Plains*. A bucolic and companionable river jaunt is replaced by a desperate, lonely, nightmare train journey. Now he was truly under the wheels.

> . . . I descended the platform like a man in a dream. It was a long train, lighted from end to end; and car after car, as I came up with it, was not only filled, but overflowing. My valise, my knapsack, my rug, with those six ponderous tomes of Bancroft, weighed me double; I was hot, feverish, painfully athirst; and there was a great darkness over me, an internal darkness, not to be dispelled by gas. When at last I found an empty bench, I sank into it like a bundle of rags, the world seemed to swim away into the distance, and my consciousness dwindled within me to a mere pin's head, like a taper on a foggy night.

In the intervening three years, Stevenson had been swept into the rapids of life and nearly drowned. At the artistic colony of Grez (so sweetly recalled in 'Forest Notes') he had met and fallen passionately in love with Fanny Osbourne. After a love-affair in Paris (where he was again dangerously ill with lung haemorrhages), she had abruptly returned to her husband in America. Heartbroken and confused, Stevenson undertook the solitary pilgrimage that became *Travels with a Donkey in the Cevennes*, and which he later said was really a love-letter secretly addressed to her.

Responding to a telegram from Fanny, Stevenson gallantly set off for America on 7 August 1879, aboard an emigrant ship, the S.S. *Devonia*. From New York he took a series of chaotic emigrant trains on the newly completed Union Pacific railroad, travelling some three thousand miles in ten non-stop days to California. He arrived emaciated, vermin ridden, penniless, and generally more dead than alive. *Across the Plains* is the record, somewhat censored, of that train journey.

Stevenson crossed America just seven years before the inauguration of the Statue of Liberty with her symbolic lamp of welcome, and thirteen years before the establishment of the huge immigration centre on Ellis Island. Yet already there were nearly a million people going west each year to seek their fortunes. He knew he was part of a historic upheaval, and his book, with its wonderful sense of unreeling space and huge displacements, reflects these pioneering hopes. Few British writers before him had observed America, with its vast prairies and enormous skies spreading before them from the roof of a rattling caboose. In his best moments, Stevenson conceived a Homeric vision of the railroads uniting the entire continent from coast to coast, 'from the Atlantic to the Golden Gates'.

But the huddled masses of the emigrants did not strike him as a romantic phenomenon. In fact what R.L.S. mostly records is the blind animal state of his fellow travellers, the terror and confusion, the moral apathy and physical exhaustion. The filth and stink of overcrowded boxcars, the crudeness of the shared sleeping and toilet arrangements, the swindling and callousness of officials and salesmen along the whole route, stunned him. For the modern reader there is also a terrible anticipation of the European refugee trains and doomed cattle trucks of the twentieth century.

The whole book has a genuinely angry tone, quite new to R.L.S. Perhaps most startling is his furious chapter on American racial prejudice: 'Despised Races'. He notes how the Chinese emigrants, having replaced the Irish as objects of national scorn, were treated as subhuman and banished to separate carriages. 'They declared them hideous vermin, and affected a kind of choking in the throat when they beheld them.' Worst of all is the attitude to the native 'red' Indians. Of the vagrant Cherokees, drunken and dressed in rags, he observed bitterly: 'If oppression drives a wise man mad, what should be raging in the hearts of these poor tribes . . .'

The final dismaying revelation, which gradually dawns upon the reader through hints and asides, is Stevenson's own broken and demoralised state. He is exhausted, feverish and sometimes close to hallucinations. His body is lice infested, with a mass of sores on his ankles, wrists and crutch. He smokes continuously, scratches himself obsessively, and takes laudanum. He has what is clearly diarrhoea. Worst of all, he begins to doubt the whole purpose of his journey. In a passage that ironically echoes the Graces' farewell at Origny, he thinks of turning back.

> . . . as we continued to steam westward towards the land of gold, we were continually passing other emigrant trains upon the journey east; and these were as crowded as our own . . . whenever we met them, the passengers ran on the platform and cried to us through the windows, in a kind of wailing chorus, to 'come back'. On the plains of Nebraska, in the mountains of Wyoming, it was still the same cry, and dismal to my heart, 'Come back!'

Only at the last does R.L.S. rise to a sudden vision of their destination, the great shining sweep of the Pacific glimpsed from the mountains: '. . . the city of San Francisco, and the bay of gold and corn, were lit from end to end with summer daylight.' Here at last was 'the good country' he had been travelling towards for so long. R.L.S. rewards the reader with a first and only hint of his romance. 'I am usually very calm over the displays of nature; but you will scarce believe how my heart leaped at this. It was like meeting one's wife.'

Stevenson arrived in Monterey at the end of August 1879. There followed a difficult and troubled interlude, living and writing hand-to-mouth in a series of cheap lodgings. He was reduced to abject poverty, sometimes living on two dollars a day. He had all his teeth removed. Twice he very nearly died, once from fever, and then from further lung haemorrhaging. Finally, he married Fanny Osbourne in San Francisco in the following spring of 1880. They took their honeymoon in Silverado, a disused silver mine on Mount St Helena above the Napa Valley. Together with Fanny's little son, Lloyd, they returned to Scotland in August 1880. His life had been transformed.

During these twelve hectic months R.L.S. achieved the astonishing feat of drafting two complete books about his travels, as well as several stories and a mass of 'Pacific' journalism. *Across the Plains* was originally conceived as the second part of his American adventure. The two parts were known in manuscript as 'The Emigrant Ship' and 'The Emigrant Train', each based on journals he had kept at the time. 'God only knows how much courage and suffering is buried in that MS,' he wrote to Sidney Colvin.

We can now see clearly how these books matured him as a man and as a writer. But the change in style, and the roughness of the subject matter, so deeply shocked his friends and family at the time that R.L.S. was persuaded to withdraw them from immediate publication. The first part, 'The Emigrant Ship', had even been set up in galley proofs by the English publisher Kegan Paul. But Stevenson's father paid £100 to have it withdrawn.

Eventually the *second* manuscript – the story of the emigrant train – was published as *Across the Plains*, in early 1883; but only as a serial in the *Century* magazine, and heavily edited. It was not issued as a complete book until 1892. The *first* manuscript of the pair – the story of the emigrant ship – was not published at all until a year after R.L.S.'s death. It finally appeared (with 30 per cent cuts) as Part One of the *Amateur Emigrant* in 1895. Here the two sections – the ship (Part One) and the train (Part Two) – were finally reunited.

Stevenson's literary advisers, Colvin and Edmund Gosse, thought that *Across the Plains* would repulse his readership and fatally lower his literary standing. They thought it would destroy the particular brand he had created: 'R.L.S.' the fantastical traveller, the whimsical stylist, the incorrigible *charmeur*. In fact it could claim to be his first truly adult book. It is the story of his journey into manhood.

Another thing changed. After this first experience of America, R.L.S. had a growing sense of himself as an international writer. In his *Silverado Journal* of 1880 he had written:

> I am a Scotchman, touch me and you will feel the thistle; I am a Briton, and live and move and have my being in the greatness of our national achievements; but am I to forget the long hospitality of that beautiful and kind country, France? Or has not America done me favours to confound my gratitude? Nay, they are all my relatives; I love them all dearly.

It was his experience of the Pacific that finally completed his transformation. R.L.S. had been dreaming about the South Seas since childhood, and his ideas were still an invalid's fantasies in his midtwenties. In a letter written from Edinburgh in June 1875, he recorded dreamily:

> Awfully nice man here tonight. Public servant – New Zealand. Telling us all about the South Sea Islands till I was sick with desire to go there: beautiful places, green for ever; perfect climate; perfect shapes of men and women, with red flowers in their hair; and nothing to do but study oratory and etiquette, sit in the sun, and pick up the fruits as they fall. Navigator's Island is the place; absolute balm for the weary.

But the final phase of his travel writing arose out of realities, and many of them harsh ones. In 1888 his health was continuing to decline. Encouraged by Fanny, Stevenson invested £2,000 in the yacht *Casco*, planning to sail from San Francisco to the Marquesas

Islands. He had literary commissions from Sam McClure's *New York World* and Scribners. This was to be the first of three such annual voyages, largely undertaken to hold death at bay.

The commission was to be his 'big book' about the South Seas, researched in a new way. It was to be illustrated with photographs, and backed by extensive reading on Pacific history, politics, languages, superstitions, missionaries, colonisation, culture, geography, imperialism and diseases. He took aboard all the instruments of research: reference books, cameras, photographic chemicals, typewriters and magic lanterns (and a banjo).

R.L.S. wanted to produce a final, great 'prose epic' of travel writing. The South Seas presented 'such a mixture of the beautiful and the horrible, the savage and the civilised'. He said his theme was nothing less than 'the unjust extinction of the Polynesian islanders by our shabby civilisation'. But below this too, perhaps, ran most deeply the idea of his own personal extinction. 'It was suggested that I should try the South Seas; and I was not unwilling to visit like a ghost,' he wrote in the opening chapter, '. . . and I must learn to address readers from the uttermost parts of the sea.'

In the South Seas is in many ways the most original book that Stevenson ever wrote. It is also perhaps the least typical. Without his usual strong sense of narrative, it is loosely divided into forty chapters, covering four of the main Pacific Island groups. Presented as a series of ocean voyages and island landfalls, it is less a continuous travelogue than a set of reflective or elegiac essays. Even its most beautiful descriptive writing is always undershadowed by a feeling of melancholy and loss. 'The first experience can never be repeated. The first love, the first sunrise, the first South Sea island, are memories apart and touched a virginity of sense.'

The persona of R.L.S. himself has distinctly changed. Sometimes he still spins a delightful yarn, as in the wonderful account of the drunken five-day festival in Butaritari. Sometimes he still winks at the reader, with the old mischievous air, as when he describes the characteristic female dress of the Gilberts.

The *ridi* is its name: a cutty petticoat or fringe of the smoked fibre of cocoa-nut leaf, not unlike tarry string; the lower edge not reaching the mid-thigh, the upper adjusted so low upon the haunches that it seems to cling by accident. A sneeze, you think, and the lady must surely be left destitute.

But more often he writes as a plain reporter, a historian, and even as an anthropologist. He describes the patterns of 'tapu' (taboo) in the Marquesas. He analyses the funeral customs of Paumotus and their accompanying night terrors. He observes the lepers of Kona. He castigates the white merchants of Honolulu. He explains the tribal legends of the Gilberts. He gives a plain, unblinking account of marriage and sexual customs in Polynesia (in the chapter entitled 'Husband and Wife'). He frequently compares the destruction and depopulation of the Pacific islanders with that of the Highland clans. He does not shrink from such subjects as infanticide, syphilis, cannibalism, drunkenness and suicide.

In the South Seas was always intended as a challenging book, and it still divides its readers. Stevenson's American editor McClure was disappointed with the material, regarding it as too controversial, without sufficient picturesque and seductive qualities. He had hoped for 'R.L.S.'s personal letters from the South Pacific', but had got only sociology. Out of fifty planned instalments he printed only thirty-seven, and R.L.S. earned only half the expected fee at £1,000.

Fanny too was doubtful about Stevenson's final rejection of his lighter, more impressionistic style of travel writing.

> Louis has the most enchanting material that anyone ever had in the whole world for his book, and I am afraid he is going to spoil it all. He has taken into his Scotch Stevenson head that a stern duty lies before him, and that his book must be a sort of scientific and historic impersonal thing . . .

Stevenson was, however, unrepentant. Amidst the long-dreamed tropical paradise, he had finally found the 'granite' globe under his feet. The modern reader may be grateful and compare Stevenson's harsh, beautiful and unblinking vision with that of another South Seas exile, the painter Paul Gauguin.

Philip Pullman on

THE ANATOMY OF MELANCHOLY,

by Robert Burton

This book is very long. What's more, like the book Alice's sister was
reading on that famous summer afternoon, it has no pictures or
conversation in it. To add to the drawbacks, parts of it are in Latin.
And finally, as if that wasn't bad enough, it is founded on totally
outdated notions of anatomy, physiology, psychology, cosmology,
and just about every other -logy there ever was.

So what on earth makes it worth reading today? And not only
worth reading, but a glorious and intoxicating and endlessly re-
freshing reward for reading?

The main reason I'm going to adduce is perhaps the least
literary. It's that *The Anatomy of Melancholy* is the revelation of a
personality, and that personality is so vivid and generous, so humorous, so humane, so tolerant and cranky and wise, so filled with
bizarre knowledge and so rich in absurd and touching anecdotes,
that an hour in his company is a stimulant to the soul. Burton (or
Democritus Junior, as he styled himself) may claim, in his brief
hundred-and-eighteen pages or so of introductory remarks, the
writer's ventriloquial privilege – ''Tis not I, but Democritus, *Democritus dixit*: you must consider what it is to speak in one's own or
another's person, an assumed habit and name – a difference
between him that affects or acts a prince's, a philosopher's, a magis-
trate's, a fool's part, and him that is so indeed' – but even if we agree
to pretend with him that the voice that speaks in these thirteen hundred or so pages is not Burton's own but that of a character of his
invention, it is nevertheless the voice of a character it's very good to
know. Those readers who have some experience of the disorder of
the mind we now call depression will know that the opposite of that

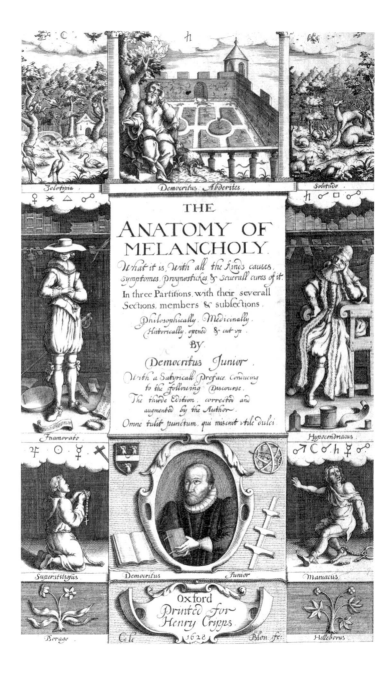

THE
ANATOMY OF MELANCHOLY.

What it is. With all the kinds causes,
symptomes, Prognostickes & severall cures of it.

In three Partitions, with their severall
Sections, members & subsections.

Philosophically, Medicinally,
Historically, opened & cut up.

BY

Democritus Junior.

With a Satyricall Preface, conducing
to the following Discourse.
The third Edition, corrected and
augmented by the Author.

Omne tulit punctum, qui miscuit utile dulci

Oxford
Printed for
Henry Cripps
1628

dire state is not happiness but energy – and energy is contagious. We can catch it from others. They cheer us up. Burton's energy is as free and abounding as that of Rabelais, and its effect on the reader is similar: an invigorating of the natural spirits (created in the liver), causing a quickening of the vital spirits (produced in the heart), leading to a stimulation of the animal spirits (formed in the brain). In other words, a tonic.

That energy is visible in the way the great onward stream of Burton's argument overflows into digressions of every kind – digressions that never settle into stagnation, but flow on to rejoin the main stream. Burton is fully conscious of this habit of his, and defends it stoutly: 'Which manner of digression howsoever some dislike, as frivolous and impertinent, yet I am of Beroaldus his opinion, "Such digressions do mightily delight and refresh a weary reader, they are like sauce to a bad stomach, and I do therefore most willingly use them" '.

The longest of these digressions is Partition 2, Section 2, Member 3, the great digression of the Air. And what an epic opening it has:

> As a long-winged hawk, when he is first whistled off the fist, mounts aloft, and for his pleasure fetcheth many a circuit in the air, still soaring higher and higher till he be come to his full pitch, and in the end when the game is sprung, comes down amain, and stoops upon a sudden: so will I, having now come at last into these ample fields of air, wherein I may freely expatiate and exercise myself for my recreation, awhile rove, wander round about the world, mount aloft to those ethereal orbs and celestial spheres, and so descend to my former elements again.

And off he goes, for thirty-eight pages, taking in 'that strange Cirknickzerksey lake in Carniola, whose waters gush so fast out of the ground that they will overtake a swift horseman, and by and by with as incredible celerity are supped up', the mystery of where birds go in winter and the possibility that they lie at the bottom of lakes holding their breath, a fossil ship with forty-eight carcasses on board discovered at Berne, showers of frogs, mice, rats, 'which they call *lemmer* in Norway', the likelihood of life on other planets, his certainty that Columbus did not discover America by chance, but because God willed it so, the similarity between the air in a region and the character of its inhabitants – 'In Périgord in France the air is subtile, healthful, seldom any plague or contagious disease, but hilly and barren: the men sound, nimble, and lusty; but in some parts of Guienne, full of moors and marshes, the people dull, heavy, and subject to many infirmities' – the desirability of building a house in a place 'free from putrefaction, fens, bogs, and muck-hills', the benefits to melancholy persons of juniper smoke, 'which is in great request with us at Oxford, to sweeten our chambers', and the importance of light and fellowship: 'wax candles in the night, neat chambers, good fires in winter, merry companions; for though melancholy persons love to be dark and alone, yet darkness is a great increaser of the humour'.

The point about Burton's digressions is not how far he roams but how firmly and certainly he comes back. He holds the whole argument in his mind, and every example or quotation or excursion grows from it organically. I mentioned the energy visible in his digressive impulses, but what keeps the whole book from bounding apart like a carelessly packed box of springs is an intellectual quality: a power of memory and comparison. In this capacity of his, he reminds me of another great Englishman, John Constable. Paintings such as *Stratford Mill* of 1819–20, or *Wivenhoe Park, Essex* of 1816, display a complexity of light and shade in which every patch of clouded shadow on the grass, every glow of sunlight among foliage, every reflection of sky in water, has exactly the value and intensity it should have next to all the rest. Constable *remembered* the colour of the reeds at the water's edge in sunlight, and the glitter of the distant façade of that white house among the trees, and adjusted them precisely to the values they would have at one precise moment under the constantly changing light of an English summer afternoon. The painting took hours, days, weeks, to make: it shows one moment, exactly. In just the same way, Burton remembers exactly where he is in his great argument, brings out precisely the right quotation, flourishes a curious story, offers a sardonic quip, and brings us back to the line of the discourse without seeming to make an effort.

And, like Constable, he does it with a dazzling quickness and dash. Close to, there is a *roughness* about each of them, which if it weren't for the marvellous intelligence in charge might even seem coarse-textured. But, in fact, it's the outward and visible sign of an inward and intellectual certainty: the power of holding an immense complexity fully and consciously in mind, and of placing each detail instantly in the light of its relations to the whole. If Burton and Constable were computers, you would say they had a great deal of RAM.

Part of this power of memory and reference is visible on every page in the overflowing abundance of quotations. Burton seems to have read everything, and remembered all of it. A wonderful example of this ability to bring out apposite examples comes early on in the Third Partition, the part of the work concerning Love-Melancholy. He begins a paragraph, 'Constantine, *de agric. Lib.* 10, *cap.* 4, gives an instance out of Florentius his Georgics, of a palm-tree that loved most fervently.' A palm-tree in love? It's impressive enough to know one example of this. But not content with citing this Constantine-who-cites-Florentius, Burton goes on to cite Ammianus Marcellinus, Philostratus, Galen, Jovianus Pontanus, Pierius, Melchior Guilandinus, Salmuth, Mizaldus and Sandys, hardly any of whom the modern reader has heard of, but all of whom, apparently, have stories about amorous palm-trees. Burton defies us to disbelieve him: 'If any man think this which I say to be a tale, let him read that story of two palm-trees in Italy, the male growing at Brundisium, the female at Otranto . . . "which were barren, and so continued a long time," till they came to see one another growing up higher, though many stadiums asunder.' The story is so charming that this reader, at least, couldn't care less if Mizaldus and Salmuth and Melchior Guilandinus and the rest were figments of Burton's imagination, and didn't exist at all. Else-where he anticipates a similar suspicion: if such examples, he says

> may be held absurd and ridiculous, I am the bolder to insert, as not borrowed from circumforanean rogues and gipsies, but out of the writings of worthy philosophers and physicians, yet living some of them, and religious professors in famous universities, who are

able to patronise that which they have said, and vindicate themselves from all cavillers and ignorant persons.

Well, I shall never know any more about Melchior Guilandinus than I have read here; but I shall never forget the palm-trees in love. And I shall certainly use the word circumforanean when I next need to refer to rogues hanging around market-places.

Burton's power of finding examples doesn't stop with other authors. He's just as ready to find plenty of examples from life. When he comes to deal with loss of liberty as a cause of melancholy, there is a passage that begins

> And what calamity do they endure, that live with those hard taskmasters, in gold mines (like those 30,000 Indian slaves at Potosi, in Peru), tin-mines, lead-mines, stone-quarries, coal-pits, like so many mouldwarps underground, condemned to the galleys, to perpetual drudgery, hunger, thirst, and stripes, without all hope of delivery!

and continues for a page or so with example after example of the miseries of imprisonment, before concluding with that abruptness that lovers of this book recognise like the quirks of an old friend, 'But this is as clear as the sun, and needs no further illustration.'

The examples he gives to illustrate his themes are often gross – some so much so that they have been kept in the sober obscurity of Latin. Others remind us of the dangers of embarrassment, such as the case of the unfortunate Dutchman, 'a grave and learned minister', who was 'suddenly taken with a lask or looseness' while walking in the fields, and compelled to retire to the next ditch to relieve himself; but being seen by two gentlewomen of his parish, 'was so abashed, that he did never after show his head in public, or come into the pulpit, but pined away with melancholy'. As if ordinary human shame weren't enough, we have to contend with diabolical possession as well, like the young maid who purged a live eel, a foot-and-a-half long, and afterwards 'vomited some twenty-four pounds of fulsome stuff of all colours, twice a day for fourteen days', before going on to void great quantities of hair, wood, pigeon's dung, parchment, coal, brass, etc. 'They could do no good on her by physic,' says Burton, resignedly, 'but left her to the clergy.'

That the supernatural should figure in Burton's great analysis is only to be expected; although the first edition of the *Anatomy* was published in 1621, just seven years before William Harvey published his treatise on the circulation of the blood and revolutionised the study of medicine, and when Galileo had established the truth of the Copernican system, the world Burton describes is firmly pre-modern. He is not in the slightest doubt about the existence of a benevolent God – atheism is 'poisoned melancholy', he tells us – or about the power of evil spirits, as in the case of the poor maid with the eel; and he's careful to acknowledge the authority of experts in the matter of goblins and other devilish beings – 'Paracelsus reckons up many places in Germany, where they do usually walk in little coats, some two foot long.'

But on the whole, there is less of that sort of thing than we might expect. 'The stars incline, but not enforce,' as he says. The greatest current in Burton's interest and sympathy is not towards superstition – 'that great torture, that infernal plague of mortal men' – but towards real human life and human feelings. After all, this is why he wrote the book: 'the chief end of my discourse', he says near the opening, is to make this great mass of material and knowledge 'more familiar and easy for every man's capacity, and the common good'.

In fact, Burton is on the side of human nature. These days, the very existence of something called 'human nature' is the subject of passionate disputation, with the evolutionary psychologists on one side and the theorists of postmodernism on the other – I would like to hear what Democritus Junior might have had to say about that debate. But there's no doubt that he knew human appetites, fears, affections and sufferings very well, and felt that the natural inclinations of men and women were to be dealt with kindly, and not suppressed: 'How odious and abominable are those superstitious and rash vows of popish monasteries, so to bind and enforce men and women to vow virginity . . . to the prejudice of their souls' health, and good estate of body and mind!'

The best evidence for his wide-ranging human sympathy comes in the great Third Partition, on love and jealousy. 'After a harsh and unpleasing discourse of melancholy, which hath hitherto molested your patience and tired the author,' he says in the Preface, he is relieved to turn to love. ''Tis a comical subject,' he admits, and in hundreds of pages and thousands of examples, he proves it to us.

His very language sparkles. The famous passage demonstrating the blindness of love begins, 'Every lover admires his mistress, though she be very deformed of herself, ill-favoured, wrinkled, pimpled, pale, red, yellow, tanned, tallow-faced, have a swollen juggler's platter face, or a thin, lean, chitty face', and continues with over a hundred epithets, to conclude 'he had rather have her than any woman in the world'. You don't write a sentence like that without enjoying it. Men don't escape, either: the absurdities of aged lechery frequently move him to eloquence. 'How many decrepit, hoary, harsh, writhen, bursten-bellied, crooked, toothless, bald, blear-eyed, impotent, rotten old men shall you see flickering still in every place?' he asks. I saw that very man myself in New York not long ago, being helped out of a limousine by a fair maid who was young enough to be his granddaughter, but probably wasn't.

On the other hand, love can work wonders with such unpromising material: 'Ancient men will dote in this kind sometimes as well as the rest; the heat of love will thaw their frozen affections, dissolve the ice of age, and so far enable them, though they be sixty years of age above the girdle, to be scarce thirty underneath.' And honest love aroused by beauty wins Burton's hearty approval: 'Great Alexander married Roxane, a poor man's child, only for her person. 'Twas well done of Alexander, and heroically done; I admire him for it.'

In fact, although the *Anatomy* shows us scoundrels in plenty, such as that oily rascal (*suave scelus*) Bishop Beventinus, who commends sodomy as a divine act, and says that tributes to Venus should be paid in no other way, and although it becomes positively Jonsonian in its dramatic power when depicting extremities of passion, as in the passage where an obsessed man, deranged by jealousy, is pictured in three pages of intensely imagined action – 'He pries into every corner, follows close, observes to a hair . . . Is 't not a man in woman's apparel? is not somebody in that great chest, or behind the door, or hangings, or in some of those barrels? . . . If a mouse do but stir, or the wind blow, a casement clatter, that 's the villain, there he is' – the great sane balance of the book is in its sympathy with ordinary human affections and sorrows and happinesses. So we have the story of the honest country fellow in the kingdom of Naples, whose beloved wife was taken by pirates, and whose willingness to become a galley-slave in order to be near her so moved the Moors that they set them both free and gave them a pension.

And this humanity of Burton's blows like a gale through the final section, on the melancholy caused by religious madness. This species of insanity, he says, 'more besots and infatuates men than any other above named whatsoever, doth more harm, works more disquietness to mankind, and hath more crucified the souls of mortal men (such hath been the devil's craft) than wars, plagues, sicknesses, dearth, famine, and all the rest'. True, it's a Protestant gale, blowing from an Anglican quarter, but we can make allowances for that; and there are things he has to say about other religions that would give a living author no end of trouble if they were newly written today, but that fact simply bears out what he says about religious madness. Blind zeal, as he says, is religion's ape. Temperance, kindness and hope make up Burton's recipe for coping with the ravages of this variety of melancholy, as of many others; and I think it is a good one.

So finally: is the book in any sense a cure for melancholy? Because it is a dreadful condition still: 'if there be a hell upon earth, it is to be found in a melancholy man's heart' is as true now as it was then. Our word 'depression' has always seemed to me far too genteel, too decorous for this savage and merciless torment. Anything that can palliate it is worth knowing; and certainly no disorder has ever had so rich, so funny, so subtle and so eccentric an anatomy. We can learn much from his psychology, which is acute and wise: 'many dispositions produce an habit' anticipates William James; his passage on the seductive pleasure of the early stages of melancholy looks ahead to some of the stories of Poe that so impressed Baudelaire, the first melancholic of modernism. His recommendation of St John's wort, whose 'divine virtue drives away devils', is taken seriously by some modern doctors, who see it as a mild but effective herbal version of Prozac; his advice to keep busy is honest good sense.

But perhaps the soundest testimony to the effectiveness of the *Anatomy* is the praise of that great melancholic, Samuel Johnson, the only man to improve on Burton – 'What is a ship but a prison?'; 'No man will be a sailor who has contrivance enough to get himself into a jail; for being in a ship is being in a jail, with the chance of being drowned' (Boswell's *Life*, 16 March 1759). Burton ends his stupendous work with the excellent advice 'Be not solitary, be not idle.' This is a great direction, says Johnson, but he would modify it thus: 'If you are idle, be not solitary; if you are solitary, be not idle.' There are many sufferers from melancholy who swear by the truth of that, and innumerable readers throughout nearly four centuries who agree with Johnson that 'there is a great spirit and great power in what Burton says'.

Nor would we wish the book a sentence shorter, or be without one of the thousands of anecdotes and quotations. This is one of the indispensable books; for my money, it is the best of all.

Roy Foster on

COLLECTED POEMS,

by W. B. Yeats

Yeats, it has been said, wrote books of poetry rather than individual poems, crafting and reshaping his work to create integrated collections, each with a distinct identity, and ruthlessly dropping or amending poems which did not suit the developing canon as he conceived it. There is enough truth in this to make the question of his 'Collected Poems' a contested arena. Should it include the poems, some of them brilliant, which are studded into his plays – or, indeed, those plays that are themselves in verse? Should it embrace poems which never appeared in, or disappeared from, his books? Should it separate out lyrical poems from those that are narrative and dramatic? Above all, should it try and reproduce the last poems in the order which he drew up for a projected individual volume, or in the order chosen by his widow and editor, and apparently canonised by the posthumous *Last Poems and Two Plays* (1939/1940), the limited-edition two-volume *Poems of W. B. Yeats* (1949) and *Collected Poems* of 1950? This last is essentially the volume which The Folio Society editors have decided to reproduce: the book which brought his astonishing *oeuvre* together, after years when much of it had been out of print due to wartime conditions and vagaries of fashion. It more or less coincided with the first major critical studies by Richard Ellmann and A. N. Jeffares, and remained a familiar vade-mecum for generations of readers as Yeats's reputation became more and more firmly established as one of the very greatest poets writing in English in the nineteenth and twentieth centuries.

For Yeats begins as a late Victorian, and the early work carries languorous echoes of Tennyson and Swinburne, as well as Spenser,

Shelley and the Young Irelanders Davis and Mangan – not to mention the translations from Irish mythological cycles which shaped his first major publication, *The Wanderings of Oisin*, in 1889. But at the same time that work announced something decisively new, in its visionary conjunctions, its unexpected but firmly controlled metre, its distinctive use of off-rhymes and unexpected assonances. Above all, Yeats implicitly announced an enterprise which he never really abandoned: a determination to exoticise Irishness, to proclaim the essential difference and originality of his country's culture. This may reflect his own uncertain status – Protestant, slightly *déclassé*, living between London, Dublin and Sligo at the whim of his splendidly Bohemian father. At the beginning of his career he stamped his work by the use of magnificently sonorous Irish names, whether of the Sligo lakes and mountains of his youth or of heroes from the sagas – as well as by a deliberate invocation of the Fenian tradition of sacrificial nationalism. His nationalist fervour cooled notably from the turn of the century, but he would continue to identify Irish cultural individuality by claiming Dublin as the home of a distinctively modern drama, focused on the astonishing plays of J. M. Synge, a constant presence in his elegiac poetry. Later, Yeats's evocation of the salty wisdoms spoken through the mouths of Irish bawds and beggars differentiates them from English bourgeois niceties; and throughout his life he claimed a place for Ireland in the mainstream of European culture (sometimes with ominous implications, as in his late poem 'The Statues') and stressed the connection of early Irish culture to ancient Egypt and Byzantium.

The other affirmation of 'difference', and indeed exoticisation, which pulses through his poetry from start to finish is a sense of the supernatural. In Irish folklore, which influenced Yeats immensely at the most formative stage of his life, the veil between the living and the dead is very thin indeed; fairies are evidence of this, in many ways, and so are the rituals and invocations of traditional country life. Yeats would combine this with a belief in a shared Universal Mind, accessed through psychic communication, ghosts and dreams: collecting folklore with Augusta Gregory, he felt 'again and again that we had got down as it were to some fibrous darkness, into some matrix out of which everything had come'. He was equally immersed in the arcane mysteries of the magical society which he joined in 1890, the Order of the Golden Dawn, where initiation involved a rite of death and resurrection. Psychic research, seances, and above all his wife's automatic-writing experiments from 1917, took up an immense amount of his attention for much of his life.

This has exasperated several critics and admirers, notably W. H. Auden, but the preoccupation brought him – as he himself said – 'metaphors for poetry'. Some of his most intriguing short poems, as well as major works like 'All Souls' Night', testify to the results. But the point must also be made that Yeats's powerful mind was by no means indiscriminatingly credulous; and that his fascination with the occult and supernatural was accompanied by a lifelong immersion in philosophical reading and speculation, particularly in Eastern religion and philosophy but also in the Christian mystical tradition, in Berkeley's thought and in Italian philosophy of the early twentieth century. The argumentative edge and bite of long poems like 'Ego Dominus Tuus', 'A Dialogue of Self and Soul', and above all perhaps 'The Tower', is evidence of this; but so is the compressed perfection of a meditation like 'Meru'. 'Genius', he wrote in his autobiography, 'is a crisis that joins [the] buried self for certain moments to our trivial daily mind.'

That current of creative argument with oneself continues throughout: Yeats, after all, defined it as one of the sources of poetry (whereas argument with others simply produced 'rhetoric', a tendency he fought against all his life). The dialogue form is very pronounced in his poetry, and creates the structure which enables a poem like 'The Man and the Echo' or – very differently – 'Adam's Curse' to present profound ideas in an accessible and even idiomatic way. The audacity of Yeats's technique develops through the following volume, along with the advancing of increasingly challenging and uncomfortable ideas about history, politics, authority, tradition and sex. It might be noted how many poems close on a question (and closing a poem is one of Yeats's consummate abilities). Even the love-lyrics of the early pages, which include the eternally popular 'He wishes for the Cloths of Heaven'

as well as 'The White Birds' and other poems addressed to his eternal goddess, Maud Gonne, are overpoweringly preoccupied with death, burial and essential solitude. This is not concealed by the 'embroidery' (his own word) which adorns them. From the turn of the century, coinciding with a number of disillusionments in his own life (including Maud Gonne's disastrous marriage), that embroidery would be consciously unpicked. Yeats declared this enterprise formally in 'A Coat', the envoi to *Responsibilities*, in 1914, but it had been under way for some time (in 1902 'Adam's Curse', again, intriguingly blended aspects of the old and the new). The distinctive new voice that comes through from around 1912 owes something to collaboration with Ezra Pound but – like Yeats's preoccupation with Japanese aesthetics, also sometimes attributed to Pound – there were clear precedents in his early conditioning.

It is clear that the landmark collection *The Wild Swans at Coole* owes much to the upheavals in Yeats's life after 1914, and especially after 1916. The Easter Rising and the development of the Irish revolution, culminating in the Anglo-Irish War and the Treaty of 1921, altered his public life, and enlisted him (if rather ambivalently) once more as the poet of nationalism. But his personal life was also convulsed, by his final attempt to make Maud Gonne marry him, his subsequent infatuation with her daughter Iseult, and then his sudden marriage – at fifty-two – to the much younger Georgie Hyde-Lees and the beginning of their supernatural experiments together. These were also the years when he decided to return to live in Ireland – partly in the ancient tower, Thoor Ballylee, which he had bought and renovated. This was only a few miles from Coole Park, home of his greatest friend Augusta Gregory, where he spent his summers from the early 1890s and which he loved above all other houses. All these themes and developments are reflected in his poetry. This is not to say that Yeats's creative writing is autobiography (even if his autobiography sometimes approaches creative writing). 'A poet writes always of his personal life,' he wrote in a 'General Introduction for My Work', unpublished in his lifetime, 'in his finest work out of its tragedy, whatever it may be, remorse, lost love, or mere loneliness; he

37

never speaks directly as to someone at the breakfast table, there is always a phantasmagoria.' Appreciation of the poems from 1916, which move from disillusionment through catharsis to revelation, is greatly enhanced by an understanding of the development of his emotional life, and his preoccupation with the great political crises of 1916 to 1922 – not only in Ireland, wracked by guerrilla warfare and military oppression, but in Russia, Italy and Central Europe.

This is the background to poems like 'The Second Coming' as well as the marvellous sequences which would play such a key part in the architecture of *The Tower*: 'Meditations in Time of Civil War' and 'Nineteen Hundred and Nineteen'. Also in the early 1920s, he was working on his extraordinary book of supernatural and historical speculation, *A Vision*, which incorporates cyclical theories of history and a scheme of archetypal personalities, based on astrology: revelation in another sense. But *The Tower* also contains 'Sailing to Byzantium', where Yeats's personal philosophy of the eternal artifice of art received its most memorable expression, and which also inaugurates one of the preoccupations of his late work: the inconsistencies, indignities and desolating insights of old age. Long before, he had referred to a section of his work as 'Poems Written in Discouragement'; from the late 1920s, his poetry is as often written in rage as discouragement, and the personae he adopts – such as Crazy Jane, with her unabashed memories of sex and her taste for abusing bishops – speak in a new language, very different from the hieratic formality of his earlier creations such as Michael Robartes and Owen Aherne. This is not contradicted by the tragic dignity of the anticipatory elegies for Augusta Gregory, 'Coole Park, 1929' and 'Coole Park and Ballylee, 1931'. But when her death did come, in May 1932, it brought Yeats first of all a severe case of writer's block, and then a determination to throw himself into what was left of life with a kind of energy and fury reminiscent of one of his heroes, Jonathan Swift.

The range, excitement and sheer nerve of the poems gathered here as 'Last Poems 1936–9' (and originally published as *New Poems* and *Last Poems and Two Plays*) were not always appreciated at the time. Some of them stem from the period when Yeats flirted with an Irish proto-fascist movement, the Blueshirts (though he quickly disassociated himself); others reflect his interest (shared by many on the right and the left) in the sinister pseudo-science of eugenics, and his disillusionment with Irish politics. There is in some of this work a kind of jaggedness inseparable from the 'late style' of some other great artists, like Beethoven or Ibsen, along with the supreme accomplishment of poems about artistic inspiration, such as 'Long-legged Fly' and 'The Circus Animals' Desertion' (a kind of artistic autobiography in verse). But there is also, intriguingly, a turning back to his earliest inspirations. Indian philosophy recurs (notably in the idea that sexual consummation can be a route to spiritual revelation); so do the ballad forms he had adopted in his very first collections, though they are now used to project challenging philosophies and assertive nationalism, rather than nostalgic other-worldly traditions. The very last poems he wrote, literally on his deathbed in the south of France, return to Irish myth and saga: ghostly armies ride out of hillsides, the return of mythic heroes is forecast, and the Irish hero Cuchulain is chosen as the poet's alter ego, to accompany him into the world of the shades.

Many of these themes, often expressed to jarring effect, are summed up in 'Under Ben Bulben', Yeats's own epitaph-poem. Drafted before many of the literally 'last poems', one of his last conscious acts was to revise and rename it. In the provisional contents page of the volume he was projecting on his deathbed, Yeats placed it first, as a kind of announcement. Though it ends with the famous epitaph he decreed for himself, this was apparently to precede the poems which came afterwards, which would be spoken, as it were, from beyond the grave. In this scheme, the poems in his last planned volume would end with 'Politics', a lovely evocation of passion above abstraction. Several recent reorderings of Yeats's *oeuvre* have reinstated the idea of ending with 'Politics', but the editors of this Folio edition have decided to reproduce the original arrangement made after his death, ending with 'Under Ben Bulben'. The inspiration for that poem came from his disagreement with Rilke's image of a poet's death as annihilation – wood consumed by flame. Yeats, by contrast, had claimed his own eternal place as a deathless golden bird singing to eternity, and at the very end of his life believed that he had – as declared in 'The Tower' –

Iain Sinclair on

THE WAR OF THE WORLDS,

by H. G. Wells

'The papers on Saturday contained . . . lengthy special articles on the planet Mars.' And so they did, Sunday too. A detail from the tag end of the nineteenth century, reported by Herbert George Wells in *The War of the Worlds* – and reprised by the *Observer* in a supplement anticipating the closest interplanetary pass in 60,000 years: at 10.51 p.m. on 27 August 2003, we, earthlings, complacent terrestrials, would feel the draught as our smaller neighbour brushed against us, at a distance of a mere 34.6 million miles. A near thing. This vision of a scarlet Cyclops watching us from the depths of brown-black space.

The anonymous narrator of *The War of the Worlds* earns his crust as an essayist, a 'philosophical writer' of the sort who might be commissioned to run up a piece for one of the broadsheets on the astronomer Giovanni Schiaparelli's speculations, published in 1877, about channels or canals on the surface of Mars, or Percival Lovell's 1896 portrayal of a dusty, merciless planet (like the Fox News depiction of Afghanistan).

Journalism, station-bookstall fodder produced by tame explainers, accelerated a democracy of information, literature for everyman. Science, to gentlemen of letters such as Henry James and Ford Madox Ford, was amusing but slightly remote – as vulgar and inessential as the technology of underground trains, telephones and internal-combustion engines. There was always a little man for such things, an oily-fingered mechanical. 'In those days,' wrote Ford, 'no one bothered his head about Science. It seemed to be an agreeable parlour-game – like stamp-collecting.'*

* Ford Madox Ford, *Memories and Impressions*, London, 1971.

Wells astonished the mandarins, the weavers of labyrinthine paragraphs, with his boisterous energy, his ability to understand, explain and exploit the substance of the contemporary world. He had emerged from nowhere, the suburbs, without family, a failed shopboy, pupil and later teacher at Midhurst Grammar School, sickly student (on a scholarship) at the Normal School of Science; a disciple of T. H. Huxley, a jobbing scientific journalist.

And then, in that miraculous period between the publication of *The Time Machine* (1895) and *The First Men on the Moon* (1901), he produced the stories, novels, conjectures, that laid out the emerging field of science fiction: interplanetary adventure, time travel, genetic engineering. The 'scientific romance' had evolved from yellowback shilling shocker, the masculine equivalent of housemaid fiction, to claim its place on the station bookstalls of captured railway suburbs such as Woking.

H. G. Wells, populist, fits neatly alongside his fictional narrator: substance and shadow. They both live in Woking and in the real world of literary agents, brothers-in-law and semi-detached wives. They keep up with current events. It's a break in the day's labour to push back the desk and stroll down to the station for the evening newspaper – with its litany of invasions, colonial wars, exhibitions, reviews of the latest novels. Like his narrator, Wells works long, regular hours. He's successful. 'In those days even philosophical writers had many little luxuries', viz. the 'pink lampshade, the white cloth with its silver and glass table furniture . . . the crimson-purple wine'.

The impact of this 1898 novel, *The War of the Worlds*, lies in its topographic verisimilitude, its forensic examination of the comfortably mundane, the complacency of Surrey suburbia, railway towns surrounded by golf links, tame heathland, somewhere to walk a dog. With his brother Frank, so Mike Ashley tells us,* Wells explored the lanes and pilgrim paths of Surrey and Kent, debating and discussing. 'Suppose', Frank remarked, 'some beings from another planet were to drop out of the sky suddenly, and began laying about them here?'

* Mike Ashley, ' "The War of the Worlds", Collectable Editions and Spin-Offs', *Book & Magazine Collector*, October 1998.

A convenient genesis for the novel, but the key word is the last one: here. The rest is a nicely developed commonplace, an adapted scare story that stays within the generic conventions of 'future war' fiction, as franchised by George Chesney in his *The Battle of Dorking* (1871). What if the Germans invaded? What if a man was gifted with invisibility? What if he travelled through time? In an imaginary Hollywood version of the H. G. Wells story, a bio-pic, this would explain the gestation of those 1890s novels: each book an idea that could be pitched, script-conference style, in a single sentence.

But Wells was also a cyclist and, less frequently, a solitary walker. In solitude, themes are broached and interrogated, minute particulars of place are discovered. 'I was walking through the roads to clear my brain,' says the demented clergyman, encountered by the narrator of *The War of the Worlds*, as he wanders the riverbank beyond an outraged Weybridge. Madness is tramped into the Thames Valley. Pedestrianism opens a dialogue, a séance between walker and landscape.

The War of the Worlds is told with tabloid speed and the lovely poetry of the commonplace: the ordinary under extraordinary circumstances. The novel's technique is posthumous and prophetic. The mood of *The Time Machine*, Wells's first novel, published in 1895, is much more leisurely, post-prandial; a Pre-Raphaelite fable with sinister shadows. Episodes unfold at their own pace, allowing space for lengthy digressions. *The War of the Worlds* happens in the world of fast news, telegrams, electricity. The false dynamic – of stock-market reports, global investments – is superimposed on slow-moving village life (pubs, horses, hedgerows). Railways are now more significant features than rivers (which prove no barrier to the advance of the Martian tripods).

Terse reportage works like radio before its time. That's why *The War of the Worlds* translated so well to America, to New England, for Orson Welles's notorious Mercury Theatre of the Air performance of Howard Koch's script. Cutting is rapid. Suspension of disbelief is immediate. The model is immaculate and can be adapted to any period at any time. Byron Haskin's 1953 film shifts the invasion to California, where the lumbering tripods become the flying saucers of Cold War paranoia.

The narrator of *The War of the Worlds* is drawn, by the instincts of a good journalist, towards the curious incident of the cylinder in the pit. Squid-like entities have been delivered by interplanetary torpedo to Horsell Common, outside Woking. This target has been carefully selected by an author who, having lived there, has a casual intimacy with the district. He knows enough, we sense, to feel that Woking deserves it. The Surrey bourgeoisie, commuters and complacent country folk, get what's coming to them.

The victims, ill-prepared grazers of newsprint, live outside the perimeter fence of London, a zone that will be made definitive by the opening of the orbital motorway, the M25, on 29 October 1986 (one day before the anniversary of Orson Welles's panic attack broadcast in 1938, and one day after the anniversary of his encounter with H. G. at a San Antonio radio station in 1940). Wells, in imagining (foreseeing) alien invasion, allows the Martians to track human movement by using their own traffic-monitoring systems: a 'thin mast upon which their restless mirror wobbled'. A prevision, clearly, of the speed trap, the insatiable dripfeed of 24-hour, real-time road footage.

The War of the Worlds foresees a future of escalating outrage, against which a numbed population is helpless. Cutting the narrator free from his safe haven, his cloying domesticity, Wells outlines a *Pilgrim's Progress* for his own times. A road novel with a respectable citizen, unhoused, walking towards London, paddling along the Thames, squatting in an abandoned suburban villa. War fever brought home. It could happen here. It will happen. This is just the beginning.

News-death. Cinema-war. Bio-terrorism. They're on the horizon, the Orwellian imperatives. 'The Tasmanians, in spite of their human likeness, were entirely swept out of existence in a war of extermination waged by European immigrants, in the space of fifty years,' writes Wells. The colonialist parallel is made. The city-grubs, churchgoers, employers of domestic servants, settled around London's ragged southern fringes, would themselves be attacked, preyed on, exterminated by invaders from a wholly alien culture. Expansionists hungry for territory and fresh blood.

The Martian cylinders land in an immaculate triangulation

45

around Woking: Horsell Common, Addlestone golf links, Pyrford. Synonyms for everything that is safe and benign and slightly boring. The heartland. The ancient dream of Englishness. Re-invaded for the first time since Gerrard Winstanley and the Diggers occupied common land on St George's Hill, near Weybridge, in the aftermath of the English Civil War.

The first cylinder sits in its sandy pit like something outrageous, a stinking fish on an immaculate altar cloth. It draws a crowd of the curious: 'a couple of cyclists, a jobbing gardener . . . two or three loafers and golf caddies who were accustomed to hang about the railway stations'. In other words, a representative sample of Surrey fauna: excursionists, hobbyists, the barely employed. This is the most desirable landscape in England, the best property values, houses and gardens customised by Voysey and Jekyll – and it has become a war zone, the front line.

Heat-Rays burning forests. 'Black Smoke' gassing civilians, drifting over Thames Valley settlements.

> An enormous volume of heavy, inky vapour, coiling and pouring upward in a huge and ebony cumulus cloud, a gaseous hill that sank and spread itself slowly over the surrounding country.

The poison gas of the First World War. Bombing raids carried out by British planes in Iraq in the 1920s. The defoliants of Vietnam. Mushroom clouds over deserts and coral atolls. The apocalyptic horrors of the First and Second Gulf Wars. Wells anticipates the hopelessness of coming ecological disaster, rivers choked with red weed. 'Charred and distorted bodies' heaped at the roadside. Shepperton destroyed by the 'pitiless sword of heat'. And, curiously, one of the first architectural casualties is a place of worship. 'The pinnacle of the mosque had vanished, and the roof-line of the college itself looked as if a hundred-ton gun had been at work upon it.'

A mosque in nineteenth-century Woking? This is not some caprice; Wells knew the ground he was describing. Look at your current Nicholson's Greater London Street Atlas and you'll find the Shah Jehan Mosque alongside the Maybury Road, right opposite the Moslem Burial Ground and the tumulus on Horsell

Common, the site of the Martian landing. Wells achieves total conviction for his fantastic tale by using accurate local detail; the loungers, jobbing gardeners, paper-boys, domestic servants, landlords who rent out horses. And only then does he unleash imagery from the Book of Revelation.

Terrified citizens, their homes devastated, take to the hills (pine clumps and mixed woodland above a chain of golf courses and railway towns). The narrator, attempting to reach London, falls in with a traumatised fundamentalist clergyman, moaning of Old Testament visions. In the distorting mirror of this extraordinary parable everything has been turned around: the aggressors in the oil wars of the twenty-first century can see the future from the other side: suburbanites shelter in holes in the ground, their armies and primitive weapons overwhelmed by a technology that has come, literally, from another planet. Confusion, panic. Guerrilla bands, under no central authority, pillaging, scavenging, robbing the dead and dying.

A Ridley Scott, mega-budget production in a late-Victorian landscape. The hundred-foot-tall tripods, war machines with their death rays, are like giant cameras, cameras that kill. Cinema metaphors convert the Thames Valley and the London suburbs into future film factories (Shepperton, Bray, Pinewood) – the perfect location for road-testing machines that scorch as they record. The flash from these weapons is like human memory burning, like an involuntary preview of Earth's last days.

The page-turning impact of Wells's narrative of invasion comes in short sharp bursts, breathless despatches, as he lays bare the three strands of time: the now-submerged bucolic past of captured agricultural land, the present of imperialism in its boastful pomp (trains that run on time, swift communication, a splendid capital city), and a vividly imagined future of endless wars, ever-improving weapons of destruction, incompetent and mendacious government, and media hungry to report everything that isn't happening. Media inventing news for satiated consumers. The Wellsian future, leaking over sandy heaths, golf courses and gently wooded hills, like a river of napalm, predicts an era when fiction and documentary will be inseparable.

Back in the 1960s, Shepperton-based author J. G. Ballard was thought to be a creator of subversive, modernist fables (fragmented and warped in homage to his mentor, William Burroughs). Now Burroughs and Ballard have been brought into mainstream culture, and Ballard's 2003 novel, *Millennium People*, has to compete with scaremongering headlines. Terror is a given, part of the human contract.

Wells, preternaturally alert, seems to have anticipated all of this. He supervises the attack on Shepperton, and the Burroughs-like notion of Martians, who are both sleepless and sexless, shooting-up with English blood. They know all about the 'physiological advantages of the practice of injection'. By subjecting a known place to such close scrutiny, Wells accesses flash-frames of events that are still to come, the warp of relativity.

The trajectory of the narrative, the hero following the River Wey down to the Thames, and eastward through Hampton Court and Richmond to London, while his brother curves around the northern rim in the direction of Waltham Abbey where the powder mills have been detonated, anticipates the defining feature of the late twentieth-century metropolis: the orbital motorway, the M25. 'The main road was a boiling stream of people, a torrent of human beings.'

H. G. Wells, scientific journalist, tale-teller, aligns himself with William Blake. 'That night the seventh star, falling upon Primrose Hill,' reasserts the sacred geography of Blake's Jerusalem.

Here Blake had the vision which he recounted to Crabb Robinson: 'You never saw the spiritual Sun. I have. I saw him on Primrose Hill.'*

Lists of place-names become, for Wells as for Blake, a litany of significance. Where the poet saw the golden pillars of his new Jerusalem set between 'Primrose Hill and Saint John's Wood', the novelist gazetted the advance of the invading interplanetary army:

* S. Foster Damon, *A Blake Dictionary*, London, 1973.

And all about him – in the rooms below, in the houses on each side and across the road, and behind in the Park Terraces and in the hundred other streets of that part of Marylebone, and the West-bourne Park district and St Pancras, and westward and northward in Kilburn and St John's Wood and Hampstead, and eastward in Shoreditch and Highbury and Haggerston and Hoxton, and, indeed, through all the vastness of London from Ealing to East Ham – people were rubbing their eyes . . . and dressing hastily as the first breath of the coming storm of Fear blew through the Streets. It was the dawn of the great panic.

The Panic in which we now live, tranquillised, amnesiac; immune to horrors – so long as they are confined to CCTV monitors and plasma-screens.

Wells has received insufficient credit as a writer of rhythmic, incantatory prose, long-breath paragraphs to cut against his tight journalistic reportage. *The War of the Worlds* makes the journey from sensationalist incident to moral parable. The long walk from Woking to Mortlake is dressed with emblematic figures: the mind-cracked clergyman, the cutlass-wielding soldier who proposes subterranean resistance. The fifth star falls on the borders of Mortlake; the rubble in which the narrator hides can be seen as a homage to the destroyed library of Dr John Dee, Elizabethan geographer and magus. The Martians are like Dee's angelic famil-iars: summoned by complacency. They are truant and unknowable.

'The wheel is absent,' the narrator remarks, when he evaluates Martian technology. And the wheel was very important to Wells. The hard-won knowledge and experience of liminal topography that underpins the fantastic narrative of *The War of the Worlds* came from cycling, that late-Victorian craze. New freedoms (for the sub-merged social classes, for women too): the open roads and lanes of Surrey and Kent. Wells was a convinced cyclist. The narrator's brother, attempting to escape a threatened London, first procures a bicycle. *The War of the Worlds* is the mirror image of the more overtly autobiographical novel Wells published in 1896, *The Wheels of Chance*.

Beginning where the fleeing Woking narrator finishes, at Putney, the cycling draper of *The Wheels of Chance* heads off into Surrey. The road is liberty. Mr Hoopdriver, the cyclist, 'felt as a man from Mars would feel if he were suddenly transferred to this planet'. Prolonged exercise and picaresque incidents bring strange dreams, dreams that form the basis of the future nightmare of alien invasion, mayhem and death.

> Nearer, nearer! It was fearful! and in another moment the houses were cracking like nuts, and the blood of the inhabitants squirting this way and that. The streets were black with people running.

As Hoopdriver approaches the ground on which Wells will stage his Martian landing, the nightmares of a bicycling tourist become apocalyptic visions. He is 'pedalling Ezekiel's Wheels across the Weald of Surrey, jolting over hills and smashing villages in his course'.

The great Wellsian push, his fictions of the last decade of the nineteenth century, can be seen as a sequence of prophetic dreams, seizures, depicting a future in which he will revenge the petty humiliations of an unprivileged childhood and troubled adolescence.

There is a cameo of the old, established Wells, lecturing his way across America, at a radio station in San Antonio, Texas, in October 1940. He meets his near-namesake, the smooth-faced prodigy who traduced *The War of the Worlds* as a hyped-up radio sensation, Orson Welles. Orson was in the last throes of shooting *Citizen Kane*, drumming up publicity and self-promoting with his usual unquenchable energy. Past slights are forgiven. H. G. Wells, global celebrity, social lion, is indulgent. The gift of prophecy, prevision, the reconstituting of future history, has passed to the new man, to new technologies.

'Very interesting,' Wells says in his curious, high-pitched voice. 'A lot of jolly good noises. I can think of nothing more desirable.' Ghosts meet. Trajectories cross. Voices of the dead are preserved on tape. The noises H. G. Wells predicted for Horsell Common, Weybridge and Shepperton are still there, always there, beneath the flight paths and reservoirs, the song of tyres, biding their time.

Helen Dunmore on

ANNA KARENINA,

by Leo Tolstoy

A novel as captivating, brilliant and protean as *Anna Karenina* eludes summary. Only its author, perhaps, would dare to belittle it with the laconic, mocking harshness which his son Ilya recalls in *Reminiscences of Tolstoy*.

> 'What difficulty is there in writing about how an officer fell in love with a married woman?' he used to say. 'There's no difficulty in it, and above all no good in it.'

This observation may be taken as a bracing antidote to the fever of praise for *Anna Karenina*, which began on its first serial publication in *Russkii Vestnik* (1873–7) and has burned ever since. However, there are deeper causes for Tolstoy's later disowning of his novel's importance. The religious and spiritual conversion which dominated the last thirty years of his life made him look back on his past with intense criticism and self-castigation. The novel which embodied that past was equally open to censure. In his memoir of his father, Ilya Tolstoy adds that he is convinced that Tolstoy would have destroyed *Anna Karenina*, if he had been able to do so. So much of Tolstoy's complex, profound inner life was irretrievably lodged in the novel. In deriding *Anna Karenina*, he might distract attention from this exposure of his earlier self.

Tolstoy's emotions about *Anna Karenina* made him emphasise the banal at the expense of accuracy. The reader's imagination immediately protests that *Anna Karenina* is not 'about how an officer fell in love with a married woman'. Vronsky is never the protagonist. The narrative pressure is almost always on Anna's side. Her thoughts and feelings, her sensuous life and her inner existence, are far more memorable than Vronsky's. The characterisation of Vronsky is not intended to draw the reader deep into his inner self; we know Vronsky's emotions well, but do not feel them to the extent that we feel Anna's. To compare Vronsky's suicide attempt with the scene on the platform before Anna dies is to realise that the characters are written in quite different ways.

Vronsky tries to kill himself because he is obsessed by the uncovered face of his own humiliation when Anna is dangerously ill after the birth of his daughter. The delirious Anna asks her husband to take Vronsky's hands away from his face so that he can see and be seen. But Vronsky cannot bear to be seen in a state of suffering and shame. He is a profoundly social creature whose sense of order and morality is governed by external standards. He must present a good face, or none at all, and the exposure to Anna's husband is a violation which he tries to wipe out by shooting himself.

Anna's death, however, is a part of her relationship with Vronsky. It is an event which flows from powerful interior causes, and from the dramatic structure of the entire novel. Certainly, Anna cares about her social humiliations and ostracism, but her death occurs not because of the way she is regarded, but because her life has become a nightmare of romantic love corrupted by insecurity, jealousy and hatred. Vronsky is never absent from her mind's eye. Minutes before her death, she longs to expose him, punish him, and yet she still wants to make him smile. Even when she sees a drunken man being led off by a policeman, she compares his desire to find escape in alcohol to her own relationship: 'Count Vronsky and I have also been unable to find that pleasure from which we expected so much.' She thinks of 'how tormentingly she loved and hated him'. The reader is deep inside Anna's sensations, thoughts and emotional understanding, and registers the confused, hallucinatory quality of her journey to the station and down the platform just as she registers them. Anna's bursts of perception, her frantic struggle to make sense of what she sees, become the only reality.

There is an ironic parallel between this scene of Anna's journey to death, where everything she sees either frightens or disgusts her, and the journey which Levin makes to Kitty's house on the morning of his engagement. Both see the world anew; one in horror, the other in bliss. What Levin sees that morning, in his uplifted and joyous state, he will never see again. What Anna sees in terror and revulsion as she walks down the platform, she will never see again.

This profound and poetic formation of patterns linking one character to another is one of the most enduring qualities of *Anna Karenina*. Sometimes the pattern is obvious, as it is in Tolstoy's working out of his theme of adultery through many different couples. Sometimes it is so subtle that it is almost concealed, as if the novel itself does not quite know how superbly it has been written. An instance is the scene in Part One, Chapter XXII where Kitty dances with Vronsky at the ball in Moscow, and 'looked into his face which was so near her own, and long after – for years after – that look so full of love which she then gave him, and which met with no response from him, cut her to the heart with tormenting shame'. Kitty's shame, and the shame which later leads Vronsky to try to kill himself, are akin. Both are to do with the exposure of deep emotion to the wrong person. Kitty does not attempt suicide, but in her weakened physical and emotional state she comes close to serious illness.

Tolstoy's handling of sexuality and adultery in *Anna Karenina* is fearless, and yet at the same time so subtly discerning that even after several readings a fresh nuance will appear. At times he draws on the broadest motifs of comedy. The opening scene, where Stiva Oblonsky wakes to find himself on the leather couch in his study because he has been turned out of his wife's bedroom, resembles a setting from *opéra bouffe*. It is the physical sympathy for Oblonsky that makes it real and remarkable. As he cuddles his pillow, remembers his dreams about decanters that were really women, and feels in the usual place for his slippers but fails to find them, there is an irresistibly childlike quality about him. Oblonsky is not innocent, but he is candid. The destructive power of his relationship with the French governess is limited, but it foreshadows the harm that will be done throughout the novel by deception and broken faith.

Tolstoy deals with these harms on two levels. One level concerns social harm, the other the wounds to the inner selves of his characters. Adultery represents the breaking of a contract not only between two individuals but between society and individual sexual desires. Oblonsky can break the contract, because he is a man and society assumes that men are driven by stronger sexual needs than women. His sister Anna might do the same, if she were willing to dissimulate. The contract must be publicly upheld, even when it is privately breached. Princess Betsy, a woman who has affairs herself and who has encouraged and connived at the secret relationship between Vronsky and Anna, will not meet Anna in public once Anna's position becomes openly irregular. Anna will be insulted at the opera, because she is living with a man who is not her husband.

The many adulterous or would-be adulterous couples in this novel seem to circle one another as in a dance. Princess Betsy has her lover Tushkevich; Oblonsky has his French governess and then his ballet-dancer Masha Chibisova; Vasenka Veslovsky pays court to the pregnant Kitty; Dolly daydreams of a romance 'with an imaginary, collective man who was in love with her'. Even the desperately sick artist Petrov falls in love with Kitty at the little German watering-place where she has gone to recover her health.

In each case the situation works out very differently. Veslovsky's flirtation with the married Kitty ends in his sudden eviction from the house, and he becomes the butt of Dolly's jokes, one more funny story to add to the layering of family life. Dolly, of course, never enacts her own fantasies. She cannot help loving Oblonsky, although her manner to him grows increasingly ironical; besides, she is a realist. With a brood of children and no money, she has no chance of an independent future. Princess Betsy is protected by her own hardened selfishness, and will go on as before. Oblonsky will do the same, although more appealingly. None of these people will give way to any impulse which may destroy them.

But Anna, of course, is destroyed, both socially and within the inner self that interests Tolstoy so passionately. In her, more than in any other character, Tolstoy explores an inward, unlimited destruction. As the novel opens, Anna is radiant with beauty, charm, self-possession, a generous spirit and the candour of a good conscience. Until she meets Vronsky as her train arrives in Moscow, her passionate love for her son conceals, even from herself, the fact that sexual passion has passed her by.

It is significant that Anna first meets Vronsky through his mother, Countess Vronskaya. The two women meet on the train from Petersburg, talk about their boys and imagine that they have formed a bond. They have, but not the one that they expect. Anna's talk about Serezha arouses all her warmest and most intense feelings, and prepares her to respond to Vronsky. Vronsky is introduced to Anna as a mother, by his own mother. He sees tenderness and kindness in Anna's face, but these qualities are absent from his own mother's face as she greets him. Countess Vronskaya screws up her eyes rather than smiling, as Anna too will later learn to do.

Tolstoy's handling of decision making is one of the most brilliant and sensitive aspects of the novel. Some characters want to believe that they have been driven by fate. Oblonsky and Vronsky both tell themselves that what has happened in their lives is inevitable: they could not have acted otherwise. Other characters insist that they live by personal choice and free will, and have to learn, as Levin does, to respect the power of the instinctive and the traditional. Anna's decisions are the engine of the novel's tragedy. Anna need not dance with Vronsky at the ball. She has not intended to dance and has completed her 'good action' (the reconciliation of her brother and sister-in-law). Kitty notices a change in Anna's face as she gives way to her impulse towards Vronsky. She suddenly sees Anna not as a good angel but as a woman who may be sensual and duplicitous, like her brother. 'Everything about her was enchanting, but there was something terrible and cruel in her charm.' Kitty is the sexually unawakened child here, made forcibly aware of the power of sexual choice in adult life.

Tolstoy contrasts the beginning of Anna's relationship with Vronsky with the events leading up to her marriage with Karenin. Anna is presented as a passive figure in her engagement, despite her beauty and charm. Her aunt, a 'rich provincial lady', was determined to marry her niece to Karenin, and 'contrived to put him in such a position that he was obliged either to propose or to leave town'. Anna, like Kitty, experiences the powerlessness of the young girl in a marriage market which she does not control. When Anna meets Vronsky she appears to make her own sexual choice, but Tolstoy shows that on a certain level she prefers to see herself as yielding

and driven. The narrative makes it clear that it isn't Anna's dance with Vronsky which is the strongest marker of future destruction, but the way she resigns her own judgement, sets aside the happiness of Kitty and then justifies her actions to herself.

There is an element of frivolity and challenge in the way that Vronsky makes his decisions. He could avoid making a young girl like Kitty fall in love with him without intending to marry her; he does not, because her emotions give him pleasure. He might treat his mare more gently; instead he rides her in such a way that he is almost bound to make the 'unpardonable mistake' which causes Frou-Frou to break her back. Vronsky appears to be in search of some extreme which he calls reality. In Anna he finds his serious, self-justifying passion, which he comes to view as his fate.

Tolstoy is extremely frank in pointing out the consequences of sexuality for the women in his novel. Dolly, for all her warmth, loyalty, humour and irony, shows the marks of her seven pregnancies in her thin hair and lined, emaciated face. Her husband feels entitled to look for sexual pleasure elsewhere, while Dolly dreads the pain of breast-feeding with cracked nipples even more than the risks of childbirth. Kitty sickens and suffers after Vronsky's rejection; even in her happy marriage she must endure a graphically described, agonising labour which the reader knows will be the first of many. Kitty, like her sister, will fade. Anna's case is the most poignant of all. Puerperal fever after the birth of Vronsky's daughter almost kills her. She learns about contraception, realising that if she is to keep Vronsky she cannot afford a succession of pregnancies. She has nothing left, she feels, but her sexual attraction.

Sickness, danger and betrayal haunt the novel. Its glowing characterisation, its masterly psychological insight, its magnificent landscapes and tender, intimate, truthful domesticity are shot through with images of loss and damage. A violent thunderstorm threatens a mother and baby; a confinement brings agony as well as joy; a fine mare is down on her back, kicking convulsively, and will have to be shot. Tolstoy takes Anna herself into depths of mental and emotional suffering which make her feel almost a stranger to her past self. Lost, alienated, afraid, Anna begins to frighten Vronsky, as well as herself.

Anna Karenina is, above all, an intensely physical novel. Changes in a character's inner life are strikingly embodied in a changed outer appearance or demeanour. Kitty alters from a fresh, vibrant young girl to a thin, sick shadow, irritable and depressed, and then back again to a young woman who has regained her force and is about to bloom in marriage, pregnancy and motherhood. Levin's tubercular brother Nicholas, with his huge, skeletal frame and big hands, is described in unsparing detail as he goes through the mysterious change from life to death. Levin himself transforms his life and physical appearance from that of a country gentleman to that of a city nobleman to that of a peasant working alongside his men. He is in constant internal flux, too; the agony he suffers over his love for Kitty in the first part of the novel is not stilled by possession of Kitty or by the birth of their son Mitya. His pain is existential and he, like Anna, dreams of death when those around him believe that he has everything to live for.

This twinning of Levin and Anna runs deep. We are let into the hearts of both with a completeness that is not matched by our intimacy with other characters. Their struggles, their inconsistencies, their sufferings and pleasures are as close to the reader as muscle to bone. We do not think about Levin; we think with him. We feel what it is like to be Anna before we can think of her objectively. Levin is horrified by his own despair when he 'should' be so happy; but the reader understands him from within. Similarly, we understand that there is no averting Anna's death. She cannot live. She is unable to love her baby daughter, because she is so intensely conscious that she has already betrayed her maternal self by leaving her son Serezha. She cannot really trust or be trusted by other women. Even Dolly, whose sympathy for Anna is rekindled, feels that there is something both wrong and sad about Anna's household.

Anna has nothing left but Vronsky, and the spectre of his abandonment of her. She understands him only too well, and realises that she is no longer a prize to him but a spoiled thing which torments him. He wants her to be as she was before he possessed her, but that woman no longer exists. By contrast Vronsky appears free, and this maddens her. Vronsky and Anna are well on the way to hating each other.

The novel's motifs of destruction come together at the end. Levin decides to live, and to suppress – indeed fight down – his vision of life's pointlessness and the call of death. Anna dies under the train. Vronsky leaves for war, as if only further immersion in a crucible of destruction will save him from the consequences of Anna's death.

Tolstoy allows this story of destruction to run its course, without a moment's fudge or softening, and yet the overall effect of the novel, while tragic, is radiant with love of life. We remember a thousand scenes: Kitty, flushed and joyous at the skating rink; Anna persuading Dolly to forgive her husband; Serezha's rosiness and his plump little legs; the making of the raspberry jam to a new recipe at Levin's estate, the naughtiness of the Oblonsky children in the raspberry canes; river-bathing, harvest and the snipe hunt; Kitty reading Levin's intentions from his mind as she chalks her reply to his proposal; Kitty not even recognising her husband in the throes of childbirth; the little peasant muttering on the dark track; the Countess Vronskaya, humanised by love and pity for her son as she tells Koznyshev that, on top of all his other sorrows, Vronsky has got toothache.

Every reader will cherish particular scenes, as the immense canvas of the novel unrolls, and the first dark drumbeat sounds beneath its shimmering surface. Only Tolstoy could find it in him to deprecate this masterpiece.

Colm Tóibín on

THE GOLDEN BOWL,

by Henry James

The first entries in Henry James's Notebooks which offer us a shadow of Adam Verver in *The Golden Bowl* appeared on 22 May 1892. James had been reading an article in the *Revue des Deux Mondes* on 'La Vie Americaine'. He began to think of somebody 'civilised, large, rich, complete, but strongly characterised, but essentially a *product*. Get the action – the action in which to launch him – it should be a big one. I have no difficulty in *seeing* the figure – it *comes*, as I look at it.'

Five years earlier, in another notebook entry, James set down the first vague shadow of what would become the 'action in which to launch him'. It arose from something which his sister Alice had mentioned to him – the story that a widower's daughter was opposing her father's re-marriage. This became the precise seed for the story 'The Marriages' which was published in 1891. The protagonist of 'The Marriages' was Adela Chart whose father was about to re-marry a woman named Mrs Churchley, much to Adela's consternation, which was partly based on the pious memory of her dead mother, but also arose from something powerful which pervades the story, Adela's closeness to her father and her sexual jealousy of the woman who had won her father's affections. The story, when it was published, pleased Robert Louis Stevenson who wrote to James from Samoa: 'From this perturbed and hunted being expect but a line, and that shall be a whoop for Adela. O she's delicious, delicious; I could live and die with Adela.' Stevenson went on to compose a number of stanzas in praise of Adela Chart. For example:

'I pore on you, dote on you, clasp you to heart,
 I laud, love and laugh at you, Adela Chart,
 And thank my dear maker the while I admire
 That I can be neither your husband nor sire.'

James, like many writers before him, including Stevenson, managed to embody in his characters themes and ideas which Sigmund Freud would subsequently formulate. Thus the idea of a widowed father and his only child, a young unmarried daughter, dramatised in a shifting set of scenes, each with an aura of something unsettlingly sexual, would have intrigued James once it occurred to him. It occurred to him for this story 'The Marriages', and once again on 28 November 1892 when he wrote in his notebook of 'a simultaneous marriage, in Paris, (or only "engagement" as yet I believe) of a father and daughter – an only daughter. The daughter – American of course – is engaged to a young Englishman, and the father, a widower and still youngish, has sought in marriage at exactly the same time an American girl very much the same age as his daughter.'

In this scenario which James set out, the father did not lose his daughter because of the two new arrivals into their family, rather they were thrown together a great deal more. This was because the daughter's husband and the father's wife already had known each other; the young husband 'would have married [the father's new wife] if she had had any money. She was poor – the father was very rich and *that* was her inducement for marrying the father.' Thus as the father and daughter spent time together, so too did the new husband and the young wife. 'The whole situation', James wrote, 'works in a kind of inevitable rotary way – in what would be called a vicious cycle.'

James went on to note that 'a necessary basis for all of this must have been an intense and exceptional degree of attachment between father and daughter – he peculiarly paternal, she passionately filial.' He saw the story as being 'a short tale' and the son-in-law as being French and poor 'but has some high position or name' and is 'clever, various, inconstant, amiable, cynical, unscrupulous'. His other three characters, James thought, would be 'all intensely American'.

Three years later, as James took stock of the ideas for new books which were in his head, he listed six possibilities, two of which he did not write, but four of which became novels. One, 'La Mourante', was to deal with 'the girl who is dying, the young man and the girl he is engaged to'; this became *The Wings of the Dove* (1902). Another he called in his notes 'The Promise' and this became *The Other House* (1896). A further novel he listed by its actual subsequent title *The Awkward Age* (1899). And one more he named as 'The Marriages', adding in parenthesis: 'What a pity I've used that name.' He summarised the plot: 'The Father and Daughter, with the husband of one and the wife of the other entangled in a mutual passion, an intrigue.' This became *The Golden Bowl* (1904).

For the reader, there is, with James, often a real fascination in attempting to find an autobiographical base for his best fiction, or in exploring why certain themes and topics continued to interest him. Nonetheless, finding characters from his life and suggesting that he based the characters in his fiction on them is often to miss the point of what he was really doing. As he imagined his books, he saw life as shadow and the art he produced as substance. He believed that language and form, the tapestry of the novel, could produce something much richer and more substantial than mere life, could produce something which offered what was chaotic and fascinating a sort of complex and golden completion.

It is often more useful to look at a drama already in the making as the seed for James's work rather than an individual character. He was interested, as his initial inspiration, in scenes rather than souls; he made his characters out of the dramatic moments he created for them, treating moral conflicts and matters of secrecy, infidelity and power with infinite subtlety. In his work a single look, a single moment of recognition, a single ambiguous resolution took on enormous force, became the fuel which powers the great engine of his novels. He dramatised the intensity in the relations between people, playing freedom against pattern, restriction against openness and dark chaos against harmony.

In the preface to *The Golden Bowl* written for the New York Edition in 1909 James apologised for the 'fewness' of the characters in the book, 'the fact that my large demand is made for a group of agents who may be counted on the fingers of one hand . . . but the scheme of the book, to make up for that, is that we shall really see about as much of them as a coherent literary form permits.'

So it is with his source material, the people and scenes that offered him enough hidden life to bring into the open. He spent August 1865, when he was twenty-two, in North Conway with his cousin Minny Temple and her sisters; they were joined by Oliver Wendell Holmes Jr and John Gray, both Civil War veterans, who admired Minny and grew to love her. James's early story 'Poor Richard'(1867) dealt with three men, two of them war veterans, one ill, who admire a single brilliant woman. More than a decade later, when he came to write *The Portrait of a Lady* (1881), he used the same configuration. A single brilliant woman is admired by a number of forceful men and another man who is ill. That month in North Conway had, it seemed, become fruitful. His cousin Minny's curiosity about the world was also to provide the seeds for his novel *The Wings of the Dove*.

In *The Portrait of a Lady* Isabel eventually married Gilbert Osmond who lived above Florence in Bellosguardo with his only child Pansy who was devoted to him. James based the rooms in a villa inhabited by Osmond and his daughter precisely on the apartment of his old friend Francis Boott, a widower who lived with his devoted only daughter Lizzie. James had first met the Bootts when they were on a visit to Boston in 1865 before they returned to Italy where, according to Leon Edel in his biography of James, 'Lizzie was reared by her father as if she were a hothouse flower, and indeed when Henry transposed her into *The Portrait of a Lady* he bestowed upon her the name of Pansy.' In a letter to Lizzie in 1874, after a visit to her father's apartment, James wrote how pleasant it might be 'to live in that grave, picturesque old house'. He added: 'I have a vague foreboding that I shall, some day.'

Osmond and his daughter would not, Leon Edel wrote, actually 'resemble Frank and Lizzie Boott; but the image of the villa, and the couple in it was to serve [James's] need in the novel that was slowly taking shape in his consciousness.' Edel went on: 'Perhaps we may discern also . . . the germ of a much later subject

. . . for in the observed relationship of a father and daughter leading a self-sufficient life, he had the theme of an ultimate novel as well.' This novel would be *The Golden Bowl*.

This infuses the Bootts and their relationship with James's art, as Lyndall Gordon has put it*. They are essential creatures for anyone considering the roots of two of James's best novels. Five years after the publication of *The Portrait of a Lady*, a shift in the Bootts' relationship offered James a seed for *The Golden Bowl*, although he would not begin the book for another seventeen years. In 1886 Lizzie Boott, still living in Florence with her father, married the painter Frank Duveneck. Soon after the wedding, James wrote to Lizzie's father introducing his close friend Constance Fenimore Woolson who was coming to Florence, asking Francis Boott to look after her there. As Lyndall Gordon has written about this introduction, James 'had no wish to promote a marriage between Boott and Miss Woolson; his interest lay in their capacities to generate an alternative world which could house his imagination.' In other words, James in London could contemplate the four of them in Florence – the father severed from his only daughter, to whom he was devoted, by her marriage, and the arrival of the outsider to offer comfort, or provide company, for the father. All four living in close proximity.

This is all a novelist needs, nothing exact or precise, no character to be based on an actual person, but a configuration, something distant which can be mulled over, guessed at, dreamed about, imagined, a set of shadowy relations which the writer can begin to put substance on, changing details, adding shape, but using always something, often from years back, that had captured the imagination, or mattered somehow to the hidden self, however fleetingly or mysteriously.

Of the many descriptions written about Henry James by his friends, or subsequent analyses of his personality, the most interesting was by John Buchan. In his autobiography, Buchan described how 'the widow of Byron's grandson asked Henry James and myself to examine her archives in order to reach some conclusion

* *A Private Life of Henry James* (Chatto & Windus, London, 1998 and W. W. Norton & Co. Ltd, New York, 1999)

on the merits of the quarrel between Byron and his wife. She thought that those particular papers might be destroyed by some successor and wanted a statement of their contents deposited in the British Museum. So, during a summer weekend, Henry James and I waded through masses of ancient indecency, and duly wrote an opinion. The things nearly made me sick, but my colleague never turned a hair. His only words for some special vileness were "singular" – "most curious" – "nauseating, perhaps, but how quite inexpressibly significant".'

James was not a moralist, although he had a special interest in morality as a kind of poetics. He relished what right and wrong looked like and sounded like; he became a connoisseur of these concepts for their shape, their aura. And of course he loved what he could do with them. Someone who, in another novelist's hands, could be presented as a villain was, once captured by James's all-embracing and all-forgiving and oddly ironic gaze, a trapped heroine until terms such as 'villain' and 'heroine' melted into meaninglessness.

This offers us a clue about James's late style. By the time he began to write *The Golden Bowl* in Lamb House in Rye in 1903, his imagination was at its most delicate and refined. His interest in the mechanics of the novel was also at its most ironic and pure. He saw the immense dramatic possibilities in withholding what was expected in a novel about treachery and discovery, innocence and experience. He saw a new shape for the novel in which, as Lyndall Gordon has written, 'manners were merely a starting point, the outermost rind of human lives. The deep structure of the great works was still, as always, allegory: evil, renunciation and the salvation of the soul.'

Yet even these terms, despite their correctness here, are too large and vague because it is essential to remember that James sought to offer them, in a tone of full and sweet understanding, to a single and frail human consciousness. Maggie Verver in *The Golden Bowl* stands only for herself. The flickering of her conscious will and her unconscious soul, and the subtlety of her responses, cannot be summarised nor easily rendered. She is made with many tones, using many patterns. Thoughts and things thus come to her in all their complexity; she deals with them accordingly. For this drama-tising of her consciousness, and of the action which takes place around her, we need a language of infinite suggestion and layered nuance.

This language enacts levels of feeling and knowing in ways which are both precise and indirect, both poetic and forensic. This late style of James suggests that feeling and knowing are open-ended and can lead, even in the bleakest circumstances, to something like forgiveness, the glossing over of unpure motives, the creation of harmony based on language as a beautiful and ambiguous way of healing pain. James came to this style gradually and by necessity not because he needed a language which was more playful and vague, but because he needed, despite all his qualms and in a way which mattered to him, a tone which was morally ser-ious, which would measure up to and mediate between the yearning of his characters for completion and the limits which life, despite all its intense variety, offered to them. *The Golden Bowl*, James's last important work of fiction, finds his talent as a stylist and as a novel-ist at its most supreme.

A. S. Byatt on

THE PINK FAIRY BOOK,

by Andrew Lang

The first of Andrew Lang's coloured *Fairy Books*, the *Blue*, appeared in 1889. Lang's biographer, Roger Lancelyn Green, himself a distinguished collector of tales, claims that 'at that time the fairy tale had almost ceased to be read in British nurseries'. He quotes Mrs E. M. Field, writing a history of children's books early in 1889: 'At the present moment, the fairy tale seems to have given way entirely in popularity to the child's story of real life, the novel of childhood, in which no effort is spared to make children appear as they are.'

Green writes of the renewed popularity of fairy tales, 'It would probably be no exaggeration to say Lang was entirely responsible for this change in the public taste.' That may have been true for generic children's stories, but the Victorian world was full of fairies, in poetry and painting, from the strange and sinister Richard Dadd to the curious fancies of John Anster Fitzgerald, and the later strange beings of Arthur Rackham.

The Edwardians, it has been observed, felt a need both for a return to an idealised childhood and for a sense that the earth was, ought to be, full of hidden folk, and strange creatures, with powers both for good and evil. Barrie peopled Kensington Gardens with fairy courts and the ghosts of dead babies. Rupert Brooke went at least ten times to see *Peter Pan* on the stage, and Shaw remarked that it was 'really a play for grown-up people'. The *Yellow Book*, with its risqué drawings by Aubrey Beardsley, carried fairy tales by Laurence Housman and Evelyn Sharp, a Fabian and feminist. Kenneth Grahame saw *The Wind in the Willows* partly as a return to the primeval world of half human, half wild creatures, like centaurs, or the shaggy-shanked godling, Pan. Kipling, in *Puck of Pook's Hill*, drew on seventeenth-century fairies, Nordic myths, and Shakespeare's *A Midsummer Night's Dream*. Our own time appears to be similar – polls for our best-loved books are headed by J. K. Rowling, Terry Pratchett and J. R. R. Tolkien.

Andrew Lang was a Scottish man of letters and an Oxford scholar. He was the author, with S. H. Butcher, of a great and influential translation of the *Odyssey*. He was poet and journalist, a student of mythology, anthropology and folklore, and author of fairy tales of his own, both in the Scottish tradition (*The Gold of Fairnilee*) and the tradition of the French courtly ladies who wrote the *Cabinet des Fées*, crossed with the burlesque of Thackeray's *The Rose and the Ring*.

As a student of folklore he was a serious polemicist, taking issue with the idea, propounded by Max Müller, that myths and folk-tales all had a single origin with an Aryan people who lived in the Himalayas. He involved himself in a dispute with Sir James Frazer about the dying god, totemism, and the nature of the relations of magic and religion. He had an interest in psychic phenomena – he saw two ghosts, and shortly before his death the Lang family death omen: 'It is black, the brute, and more like a cat than anything else; but horrified percipients add, with a shudder, that whatever else it may be, it is only superficially feline, and of no known species of the animal kingdom.' He was, however, sceptical about table-turning, ectoplasm, and spirit-messages through mediums.

Lang came to folk-tales as an anthropologist. He wrote:

The natural people, the folk, has supplied us, in its unconscious way, with the stuff of all our poetry, law, ritual: and genius has selected from the mass, has turned customs into codes, nursery tales into romance, myth into science, ballad into epic . . . The student of this lore can look back and see the long-trodden way behind him, the winding tracks through marsh and forest and over burning sands. He sees the caves, the camps, the villages, the towns where the race has tarried, for shorter times or longer, strange places many of them, and strangely haunted, desolate dwellings and inhospitable . . .

When he first began to collect folk-tales he had the folklorist's professional distaste for authored and decorated tales. He also distinguished between myth and folk-tale – in *The Blue Fairy Book* he included the myth of Perseus and Medusa but recast it in an anonymous folk-tale form, turning Perseus into a generic and nameless 'the boy' and the nymphs of the Hesperides into 'the Western Fairies'.

The brothers Jacob and Wilhelm Grimm published seventeen versions of their *Children's and Household Tales* between 1812 and 1864. Their idea was to record orally told stories and to restore nineteenth-century versions to an 'original state' which they believed would reveal the forms of an ancient German religion and culture. They made collections also of Old Danish heroic songs, 'Old German Forests' and Irish fairy tales. Jacob wrote histories of the German legal tradition and of the German language, and an encyclopaedia of German mythology. Modern scholarship has shown how Wilhelm smoothed and rewrote the raw story material sent by Jacob, and has also suggested that the wise old Marie who recited the traditional tales was in fact a young woman of Huguenot descent, who knew the French fairy tales of Perrault. But the 'feel' of the Grimms' collections has that sense of simultaneous wonder and matter-of-fact that recurs in folk-tales from all over the world, and is quite different from the courtly, playful – and moralising – voice of the French storytellers, from Perrault to Madame d'Aulnoy. As readers or hearers we are both amazed by the uncanny, and calmly expectant of the satisfactory ending we know will come. There is no aesthetic experience, no literary experience, quite like it. It is finding one's mind trapped in a shiny web of endless, shape-shifting, self-resembling links.

In 1893 Marian Roalfe Cox, under the auspices of the Folklore Society, published a book containing three hundred and forty-five variants of the related fairy tales of Cinderella, Catskin, and Cap o' Rushes. A motto, presumably of the Folklore Society, *Alter et Idem* (Different and the Same) appears, with a woodcut of a leaping, hooded, round-bellied, booted figure brandishing a flame, on the title page. The Introduction is by Andrew Lang. In it he discusses the problems of transmission and repetition of motifs and episodes in tales from all over the world. He appears to be arguing that story-tellers both repeat types by rote *and* spontaneously vary incidents and objects. To illustrate his point he makes up a tale of his own on the spot.

Let us try a fancy combination. We may begin with the childless pair, the child magically conceived. Let the mother die, leaving a dog to daughter [*sic*]. The father remarries, has two daughters, they spite the first girl. They are sent one by one to accomplish some feat, by the dog's aid the first daughter succeeds. She is rewarded with the gift of a palace with a Bluebeard chamber. Her sisters urge her to open it, she finds an enchanted young man in the form of a statue. She revivifies him, they fly and are pursued – the usual 'magic flight'. She is never to call him by his name, she does so; he forgets her and is betrothed to her eldest sister. By dint of presents provided by her dog, she gets leave to cook a cake for him, and leaves her ring in the cake. He swears he will only marry the person whom it fits. Her sisters nip and clip their fingers in vain. The dog remarks that the true owner is in the kitchen. She is discovered and married to her lover.

What tale is that? Under which type is it to be grouped? Such a combination is perfectly possible, and it may perhaps be difficult to put a name on it. But tradition supplies abundant examples nearly as indeterminate. I suppose then that storytellers have always been making combinations . . .

Here Lang is arguing against over-rigorous scientific analysis of 'tale-types', and for the recognition of the complexity and variety of the retelling of the repeated incidents. I at least responded to his 'fancy combination' partly with pure narrative curiosity – how would *this version* be worked out? Skeletons of folk-tales or fairy tales are curiously gripping because folk-tales themselves have a two-dimensional quality. Their world is full of narrative energy, but there are things they don't do. They don't analyse feelings. They don't deal in hope or grief or desire. Their magic is curiously matter-of-fact.

The best analyst I have read of the way in which these stories work is the Swiss scholar, Max Lüthi. In his book *The European Folktale: Form and Nature* he isolates the peculiar glittering quality of these stories. His chapter headings read 'One-dimensionality', 'Depthlessness', 'Abstract Style', 'Isolation and Universal Interconnection' . . . He discusses the strange isolation of the characters – the only child, the youngest son, the stepdaughter, the orphan. Kings and poor men, dancing girls and simpletons, golden boys and girls in radiant dresses don't come from communities, or have complex relations with other human beings. Things too are isolated – gold, silver, diamonds, seeds, nuts, swords – and come into play only when the story needs them. A hero, he points out, will suddenly remember a magic gift he has been given, or a beast he has helped who may prove useful, only at the point in the plot when these are required – they then disappear, are not thought of again. Lüthi is particularly good on the restricted colour range of the fairy tale. The folk-tale, he says, 'prefers clear, ultrapure colours; gold, silver, red, white, black, and sometimes blue as well'. Green, he says, is 'strikingly rare' – the folk-tale forest is a large forest, a dark forest, practically never a green forest. The folk-tale likes isolated glittering objects – a golden key, a golden spinning-wheel, a glass mountain. It creates – and this is a major perception – a world where everything is defined and isolated, like bits of mosaic, and therefore part of a universal pattern which can be felt to exist beside, or under, or through the natural world. We all seem to respond to, and need, that.

Lüthi is also particularly helpful with the problem of pain, violence and cruelty steadily raised by critics fearful of exposing children to the world of the Brothers Grimm. He points out that the principle of neatness and isolated two-dimensionality applies to violence and death. People are 'cut to pieces' or 'split in two' – 'we see the symmetrically and sharply sundered halves, from which no blood flows and which lose none of their precision of form'. A princess may have her hands cut off and hung round her neck and be put into a boat and pushed out to sea. When she is rescued her hands will be miraculously restored. An animal helper will urge the hero to cut off its head and will be transformed into a boat. The

punished witch rolling down a hill in a barrel stuck with nails is imagined only so far, as a motif. As is a foolish man tied in a sack with a heap of stones, thinking he will find magic cows at the bottom of the lake.

These latter examples did worry me as a child. My imagination almost – but not quite – touched on the nails ripping the flesh, on the choking water flowing into the sack. W. H. Auden, in an introduction to a collection of tales from the Grimms and Hans Andersen, took seriously the 'charge against fairy tales, that they harm the child by frightening him or arousing his sadistic impulses'. An experiment would be needed, he wrote, to see whether fairy-tale listeners were more sadistic than others. 'As to fears,' he wrote, 'there are, I think, well-authenticated cases of children being dangerously terrified by some fairy story. Often however, this arises from the child having only heard the story once. Familiarity with the story by repetition turns the pain of fear into the pleasure of a fear faced and mastered.'

I am not quite sure it works exactly like that. Auden's requirement of repeated readings touches on another aspect of tales told to children. They like to hear them over and over, and they like the words to stay exactly the same – they object if the teller cuts, or embroiders, the tale. This too hints that the essential pleasure of the listener is linked to the rigorous formality of the arrangement of the elements of the tales – to Lüthi's recognition of a rigorous 'abstract style'.

Lang in his Preface to *The Pink Fairy Book* raises the question of frightening children, with reference to the Danish tale he includes, 'The Princess in the Chest'. *The Pink Fairy Book* is not a strict collection of folk-tales, or Märchen. It includes authored tales, three by Hans Andersen, including 'The Snow-Queen', one of the greatest stories ever written, and the fanciful 'Princess Minon-Minette' from the *Bibliothèque des Fées et des Génies*. The stories are an eclectic mixture in other ways – there are tales from Africa and Japan, as well as from northern and southern Europe. Tales are translated from translations – the Sicilian story is translated from a German translation, the African tales are translated from French. Hans Andersen himself is translated not from Danish but from the German, as was usual in Victorian England – recent work on the translations suggests that he was smoothed and sentimentalised as the translations succeeded each other. The translation of the Sicilian story – 'Catherine and her Destiny' – may, I think, disguise the fact that the Italian word for what we call fairies or elves is 'Fata' – a Mediterranean kind of spirit who is both fairy and fate. Lang employed many translators, including his wife. It resulted in the stories changing shape in transmission as stories do.

But in the case of 'The Princess in the Chest' Lang thought it worthwhile to explain some changes he had made to the Danish tale – which, he says, 'need not be read to a very nervous child, as it rather borders on a ghost story. It has been altered, and is really much more horrid in the language of the Danes, who, as history tells us, were not a nervous or timid people.' The distinction between ghost story – designed to arouse fear and anxiety – and fairy tale is interesting. Danish friends sent me a text of the original and translated the ending, whose omission seems to be the striking difference in Lang's version. Lang ends with a wedding and happiness ever after. The original ending reads:

> But many years later, when all the tiles in the church had to be relaid, a loose stone was found in the middle of the floor. Beneath a huge vault was found in which lay the bodies of the sentries who had watched the coffin of the princess. Each neck had been broken. This was the work of the evil being who had possessed the princess, and had drunk three drops of their blood every night.

Lang is right – this vampiric shiver is stronger than a fairy-tale emotion, and the suggestion of a possessing evil being is a motif that belongs more to a ghost or horror story than to a fairy tale. Hans Andersen creates the same shiver with a bewitched and evil princess in 'The Travelling Companion'.

Andersen's tales do and don't resemble the forms of the traditional fairy tale. He understands these forms from the inside, but he does not restrict himself to depthlessness, abstract style or isolation. Indeed, I believe he was the first writer to invent the form of tale in which inanimate objects – darning needles, bits of broken glass, or, in the ones included in *The Pink Fairy Book*, a conceited shirt-collar, a flirtatious garter, and a dancing pair of scissors – all have more personality than they can manage, and are comic and tragic by turns.

When I was a child, I read fairy stories indiscriminately, in collections like *The Pink Fairy Book*, and did not at first distinguish between authored tales and traditional ones – I was just greedy. I think one of my earliest discoveries, that went to making me a writer, was that Hans Andersen was an author, with his own purposes and intents, one of which – I was deeply shocked – was to make me, the reader, disturbed and unhappy. Reading 'The Little Mermaid' with its agony, and its unsatisfactory, un-fairy-tale ending, disturbed me deeply – but I couldn't avoid it, I knew it was good and important, I kept going back to it. The same was true of 'The Snow-Queen'. It is true that this has a happy ending – but it also has real fear and pain, a real sense of alienation when Kay is the prisoner of the beautiful Snow-Queen. The characters are characters, with passions – including the wonderful robber-girl, who would not have had any character in a true fairy story. Andersen is playing with the counters of the true tale – the glitter of ice and slivers of broken mirror, the quest to find the lost and stolen brother, the witch who catches Gerda, the animal helpers, the magic journey, the magic word that releases the prisoner in the ice palace. But everything in Andersen has feelings, has individuality, is briefly completely alive. It is true – and this is something that bothered me as a child – that he can be sentimental and moralising. Reading him is difficult – something too sweet is laid over a real apprehension of cold, threatening and frightening things. Through finding what I did and didn't love in him, I saw more clearly the power of the anonymous tales that simply tell themselves, in their bright, inevitable world. The tales affirm that courage and persistence will always be rewarded, that a generous spirit has nothing to fear. Andersen knew better. He wrote fairy stories and understood tragedy and terror. We need both. Which is why an eclectic collection like this is such a pleasure to read through.

Frances Wilson on

ADVENTURES OF CASANOVA,

by Giacomo Casanova

Giacomo Casanova saw his life as a comic performance in which he played the lead role. At least this is how he portrayed his many adventures in his monumental memoir, *Histoire de ma Vie*, which was, he explained, 'nothing more than a satire of myself'. Satire uses its irony to make a serious point, which for Casanova was to record for posterity his unique views on love. 'I love myself', he said of the remarkable figure who took centre stage in every scene of the 3,600 pages he produced, 'more than I love anyone else.' His *Histoire* is a celebration of a man who deprived himself of nothing, and of a life lived for pleasure alone.

Born the son of Venetian actors in the Calle de Commedia in 1725, it is perhaps not surprising that Casanova casts himself as the hero of his own drama. Role-playing was in his blood and eighteenth-century Venice, city of masquerades, with its clash between carnival mayhem and patrician oligarchy, contained all the ingredients necessary for comedy of the kind at which Casanova excelled, whereby a handsome rogue charms his way into high life and low, and no one is ever who they seem to be. Casanova was happiest around disguise – his most important lovers, such as the castrato Bellino, the nun 'M.M.' and the cross-dressing Henriette, each wear concealing costumes of some sort – and he would always gravitate towards women who could perform, in both senses, with as much enthusiasm as himself.

The fact that the *Histoire* was written at all is dramatic. Now a melancholic and homeless old man, expelled for the second time from his beloved Venice, Casanova accepted the position of librarian for Count Waldstein at Dux Castle in Bohemia. He had nowhere left to go and nothing left to do; his purse was empty, his sexual energies had long since been spent, and many of his former friends, lovers and patrons had died. While his own life had become, for the first time ever, silent and predictable, the French Revolution was reshaping the Enlightenment world he had known so well. For someone who had enjoyed the most dazzling cities of the West, who had embarked on a battle of wits with Voltaire and moved in the court of Catherine the Great, the bathos of ending his days a virtual prisoner in a dark and unknown corner of Europe was hard for him to bear. 'Writing my memoirs was the sole remedy I believed I possessed to avoid going mad', he wrote at the close of the manuscript on which he had worked with feverish energy for eleven hours a day, 'or dying of sorrow from the unpleasantness to which I was subjected at the hands of the rascals living in the castle.'

He wrote to keep himself sane but also to escape, as he had done once before from the Leads of the Doge's Palace where he was imprisoned, and it is as a triumph of imagination more than a curriculum vitae that we must see the *Histoire*. His memoirs, written in French rather than Italian so they would be more available to readers, enabled Casanova to impose himself once more on the stage of European culture; had he not produced his masterpiece he would have come down to us as just another libertine, ducking and diving and pushing his luck. It was the *Histoire* that gave shape, structure and significance to his fifty years of peripatetic wanderings and chance encounters, the *Histoire*, as opposed to anything else he achieved, that made his reputation.

But the image we have of Giacomo Casanova is not quite the one he constructed himself. It is the role of lover with which he is overwhelmingly associated – according to the *Histoire* he slept with around 120 women – but there were many other parts he chose to play. He was, for a while, a soldier, a violinist, a nobleman, an entrepreneur and a spy; throughout his long life he was a philosopher, a gambler, a writer of ambition and a gourmand ('I have always liked . . . cheeses', he says in the *Histoire*, 'whose perfection is reached when the little creatures which inhabit them become visible'). But the role in which he excelled, and the one which demanded his most brilliant performances, was that of the confidence trickster. When Casanova determined to deceive with his quack medicine and his fake magic, he played on the weakness of his victims; but when he set out to seduce, it was strength he looked for in his women – strength of smell as well as character: 'I have always found that the one I was in love with smelled good,' he recalled, 'and the more copious her sweat the sweeter I found it.'

Casanova the con man made fools of those he thought fools anyway, but he never seduced a woman without believing he loved her first, and never knowingly misled anyone for whom he had fond feelings. As a comedian, he preferred his endings happy ('sadness is a disease which in the end kills love'), but it was the beginnings he enjoyed the most, and he gives more attention by far to the chase than to the consummation. His attempts to seduce Bettina, Bellino, 'M.M.' and Marie Charpillon are recorded in painstaking detail, and once a seduction has been achieved, the torrent of words dries up. The only time Casanova is ever euphemistic is when he describes the act of sex itself. His literary style can be summed up by his own phrase, 'the interest of the thing is in the details'; whether he is describing his escape over the roof of the Doge's prison, which took him two hours to relate in company, or his visits to the nunnery at Murano, it is the building up of suspense at which he excels.

When Casanova's mother, Zanetta Farussi, eloped with Giatona Casanova, an actor and dancer, her father, who was a shoemaker, died of shame; such was the status of the acting profession into which Giacomo was born one year later, when Zanetta was seventeen. Despite being drawn throughout his life to actresses and singers, the lowliness of his birth was a mantle he quickly threw off. Casanova believed, however, that his origins were not as humble as they seemed and that his real father was the aristocratic Michele Grimani, who owned the San Samuele Theatre where his mother was employed. It was also rumoured that Francesco, Zanetta's next child, was the son of the Prince of Wales, who later became George II.

Zanetta's work took her all over Europe, so it was Casanova's grandmother, Marzia Farussi, who raised the young Giacomo and his siblings. Despite the old woman's evident kindness and his own remarkable memory, his early years are shrouded in forgetfulness. Casanova writes that he can recall nothing of his life until he was eight, and this first memory, which anticipates much of what his life will contain, is of powerful and mysterious women who cast spells over his naked body. To cure a heavy nosebleed, Casanova's grandmother took him by gondola to the island of Murano, where he met a witch with a black cat in her arms who locked him in a chest. When he was let out, his nose had stopped bleeding and the witch told him to undress and lie down while she recited spells. A 'charming lady', the witch predicted, would visit him the following night, which indeed she did. As he lay in bed, he writes, he saw 'a dazzlingly beautiful woman come down by the chimney, wearing a huge pannier and a dress of magnificent material, with a crown on her head set with a profusion of stones which seemed to me to be sparkling with fire'. The 'fairy' emptied the contents of several small boxes on the child's head, muttered some words, kissed him and left. Casanova's grandmother swore him to secrecy.

Soon afterwards his father died, leaving Giacomo under the protection of the same Michele Grimani whom he believed to be his real father anyway. Comic coincidences such as this are a feature of the picaresque world of his memoirs, in which he almost marries a woman he discovers to be his own daughter and he is bound to bump into an old lover again, at a concert or in a coach, in a different country and under a different name. The eighteenth-century Europe he describes is the size of a bustling marketplace.

Aged nine, Casanova was sent to Padua to live with a tutor, Dr Gozzi, and here he fell in love for the first time, with Gozzi's young sister Bettina. After leaving the Gozzi household in 1727 he enrolled at Padua University, where he reluctantly studied law, having been told that he had the rhetorical skills of a successful lawyer. Casanova's interests lay more in medicine than law, and he continued to pursue his interest in cures and potions. Following the death of his grandmother, he lost his base in Venice and began the

peripatetic existence that would define the first half of his life. In 1755 a decade of shady dealings, including dabbling in the Cabala and in alchemy, caught up with him and he was imprisoned, aged thirty, in the prison known as 'the Leads', at the top of the Doge's Palace. It was from here that he made his famous escape, at which point he began to see himself as invincible. In Paris, where he then lived, he became a millionaire when he helped to found the state lottery, following which he involved himself in a long-drawn-out confidence trick in which he persuaded an elderly widow,

Madame d'Urfe, that she would give birth to herself in the form of a boy, who would be conceived during intercourse with Casanova himself.

His travels took him to London, where his former lover, Teresa Imer, was living with their child Sophie. London was the only city by which Casanova was defeated, and when he left, in danger of being hanged for a false bill of exchange, the melancholy that would dog him for the rest of his life had begun. He then visited Germany, where he met Frederick the Great, and St Petersburg, where he met Catherine the Great. A duel and a further prison sentence later, he was living in Trieste when he finally received the pardon by the Inquisition that allowed him to return to his beloved Venice. But both he and the city had changed during his nineteen years of exile, and Casanova did not find again the happiness of his youth; he had a tepid affair with a simple woman and, after eight disappointing years, was expelled again, this time for publishing an attack on the patrician society of the Republic. Aged fifty-seven, Casanova was back wandering around Europe, pausing only when he met a fellow Freemason, Count Waldstein, who offered him a job as librarian in his Bohemian castle. With no other options, Casanova accepted the post and for the following thirteen years he devoted himself to his writing, specifically his memoirs. He died aged seventy-three in 1798, the same year that Wordsworth and Coleridge published their *Lyrical Ballads*, thus closing the door on the eighteenth century and ushering in the age of Romanticism.

The only woman immune to Casanova's charms seems to have been Zanetta. The sickly, needy child of a beautiful, scornful and absent mother, Giacomo spent his life trying, again and again, to fill the void left by the absence of her love. His nose bled throughout his childhood, and rejection would always make him ill. In this sense, Casanova's sexual relationships seem motivated less by the pursuit of pleasure than by the avoidance of pain. More often seduced than seducing, he describes himself as the pawn of women who continually run rings around him. He was rejected by his first love, Bettina, and again by La Charpillon. His harrowing experience with La Charpillon brought to a close what he called his 'first act'. When he finally realised he had been her dupe – and that for once he was the victim rather than the perpetrator of a confidence trick – he considered taking his life. Such scenes show that he could play the tragic hero when it was required of him, but Casanova was never in this genre for long.

While he liked his women to be as ripe as a swelling cheese, they nonetheless remained for Casanova figures of fantasy rather than flesh and blood. He describes the women he loves as devoid of jealousy or petty grievance, as endlessly generous, both sexually and emotionally, and always prepared to let him go when the time has come. When, for example, he is involved with two nuns from the same convent, the discovery of his infidelity causes nothing but delight, and the women celebrate by inviting their lover to share them both together. This episode is the closest Casanova comes to writing in the genre of erotic fantasy, and while there is very little in the *Histoire* that could be called pornographic, the world he likes best is the Utopia we find in pornography, in which sensual pleasure stops the clocks and whatever lies beyond the body fades into insignificance. He was always upset by the intrusion of reality, as when the idyll he shared with Henriette came to its inevitable end, and she returned to her life in France.

Henriette was for Casanova the perfect woman: 'Who can this girl be,' he asked on first meeting her, 'who combines the finest feelings with an appearance of the greatest libertinism?' Her appeal to Casanova was less her combination of fine feeling with libertinism than the mystery surrounding who she was: mystery was an aphrodisiac to Casanova, and the question of Henriette's identity would fascinate him all his life. Henriette also contained the type of intelligence he liked in a woman. 'The intelligent woman who cannot make a lover happy is the bluestocking. In a woman, learning is out of place; it compromises the essential qualities of her sex . . .' Instinctively sharp and perceptive, Henriette's femininity was uncontaminated by formal education or intellectual ambition:

A beautiful woman without a mind of her own leaves her lover with no resource after he has physically enjoyed her charms. An ugly woman of brilliant intelligence makes a man fall so much in love that she leaves him feeling no lack. So what must I have been with Henriette, who was beautiful, intelligent and cultivated? It is impossible to conceive the extent of my happiness.

Henriette made Casanova happy because, with 'never a moment of ill-humour, never a yawn, never . . . a folded rose petal . . . to trouble our content', she left him 'feeling no lack'. She fulfilled him physically and intellectually, but she also filled the emptiness left in him by Zanetta, and when their relationship ended, Casanova took to his bed like a child.

Along with Zanetta and Venice itself, Henriette was to be the great love of Casanova's life. She merged into the languid, serpentine city and the distant, beautiful mother to form, in Casanova's imagination, the perfect woman – inscrutable, enticing, eventually rejecting. As W. H. Auden said of another lover of Venice, Frederick Rolfe, the republic was 'the Great Good Place . . . built by strong and passionate men in the image of their mother, the perfect embodiment of everything he most craved and admired, beauty, tradition, grace and ease'.

Even on his deathbed in Bohemia, Casanova was waiting for the Inquisition to give him a final pardon. He could then take his encore and return, one last time, to the place of his birth.

Peter Ackroyd on

OLIVER TWIST,

by Charles Dickens

Oliver Twist was born in the pages of a monthly periodical entitled *Bentley's Miscellany*. He emerged, to be more precise, in the second number of that journal – dated February 1837 – under the title 'The Progress of a Parish Boy'. The novel had begun almost by accident, as a series of articles concerning the imaginary town of Mudfog, but as soon as Dickens had hit upon what he called the 'capital notion' of the workhouse child, the narrative took shape before him. He may in fact have been considering such a plot, or something like it, for some time. Four years before, he had been talking about 'a proposed Novel' even as he began writing his earliest stories and sketches, and the notion of a poor child rescued from poverty and distress is likely to have had an early and immediate appeal for him. It was, after all, part of the history of his own life.

Before beginning *Oliver Twist* in serial form, however, he had already been buoyed by the success of *Sketches by Boz* and the monthly numbers of *The Pickwick Papers*. Within the space of a year he had become the most famous writer in England. Nothing quite like it had happened before or since. Yet even as he continued to write *The Pickwick Papers*, he embarked upon a new novel, *Oliver Twist*. He had just left the reporting staff of the *Morning Chronicle* and had calculated that he now had the time and opportunity to concentrate upon his more important writing. But he had also just been appointed the editor of *Bentley's Miscellany*, the periodical in which the new novel was to be serialised, so he was busily engaged on a variety of other business, such as commissioning and proof-reading articles. He would remain in that state of restless energy and furious production for the rest of his life.

George Cruikshank

There has been some controversy over the origins of Oliver. The rebarbative George Cruikshank claimed that he was the principal begetter of the parish boy's progress. Cruikshank was the illustrator of the series, and in his depiction of such notable protagonists as Fagin and Bill Sikes he may have originated something of their respective characters. It was once said of Cruikshank's drawing of Fagin in the condemned cell that it was so realistic, it might have been drawn by Fagin himself. But it is unlikely that the artist played more than a provisional role in the conception of the narrative.

The true source lies somewhere within Dickens himself, if only because the childhood of Oliver Twist is so close to his own. The story of Oliver is the story of the orphan's slow and bewildering ascent from the dirt and uncleanliness of the London streets to the bright world of gentility and respectability. The history of Charles Dickens's own childhood – the forced descent into work in Warren's blacking factory and the incarceration for debt of his father in the Marshalsea prison – is too well known to need rehearsing here. But the important point is that some of the salient facts of Dickens's childhood misery are carried over into the fictional narrative. The 'dark and broken stairs' of Fagin's den beside Field Lane is a simulacrum of the rotten stairs in the blacking factory. The name of Fagin himself is derived from one of the young Dickens's workmates in the blacking factory by the Thames. The child's name was Bob Fagin, and he seems to have befriended Dickens in his agony and distress. Yet Dickens seems to have felt horror rather than gratitude – horror at his association with a common boy who taught him the tricks of the blacking trade. So the name of Fagin was attached to one of the most egregious villains of the nineteenth-century novel. The workings of Dickens's imagination were strange indeed.

It is perhaps strange, for example, that he was able to write *Oliver Twist* at the same time that he was composing *The Pickwick Papers*. Some of the most comic episodes of the picaresque novel were being written in the same week – and indeed on the same day – as some of the most poignant and plaintive paragraphs of its counterpart. They were, in fact, quite different pieces of work. *Oliver Twist* was in part written as a polemic against the conditions of the early nineteenth-century world. It should be recalled that Dickens was one member of a radical generation growing up in the 1830s, which was filled with social optimism and a belief in political reform. In fact, he had opened up the pages of *Bentley's Miscellany* for their contributions. The early chapters of *Oliver Twist*, for example, were specifically aimed at the abuses and defects of the New Poor Law that had been introduced three years before. Some of its measures were designed to 'rationalise' on Benthamite lines the regime of the workhouses, thus aggravating the misery endemic to such places. Dickens directly satirises the new dietary provisions of the Law with Oliver's cry for 'some more' supper. He was 'desperate with hunger, and reckless with misery', and in that short appeal he embodied all the horrors of a system designed only to grind down the poor and the destitute with the burden of their own misery. *Oliver Twist* was aimed at the very heart of a generally uncaring society. It has often been said that this was the first novel that has a child as its central character. That is true enough, but it is also significant as the first novel in which a suffering child – a victim of the public world – is made audible and visible to a large general audience of readers.

So *Oliver Twist* is created from personal experience and public polemic mingled together. Dickens was a journalist before he was a novelist, and in this book the twin powers of description and imagination animate a story that still has the power to move and enchant. He wrote it quickly and fluently, as if his whole life were somewhere within it. There are descriptions of his coming down to the drawing room in Doughty Street, where he lived with his young wife Catherine, and continuing to write even as the assembled company of guests carried on talking and laughing. He was convivial even as he worked. He said at a later date, of one effect in the novel, that 'it came like all my other ideas, such as they are, ready made to the point of the pen – and down it went'. There were other sources of inspiration close to hand. Just five minutes' walk from his middle-class house in Doughty Street were Field Lane and Saffron Hill, the very dark areas of the city he was even then bringing to life. It was one of his often-stated beliefs that, in London, luxury and degradation, riches and poverty, lie side by side. He lived, as it were, beside Fagin and his wretched children.

But then the conviviality of the house in Doughty Street was shattered forever. On 7 May 1837, his sister-in-law died from a sudden failure of the heart. Mary Hogarth was seventeen years old, and had been devoted to the young Dickens. He returned the attachment, and her sudden death provoked in him a sense of loss and grief more powerful than any he had ever before experienced. He was unable to write that month's episode of *Oliver Twist*, but her demise affected the novel in other ways. From this time forward, it takes on a different tone. When he returns to work at the beginning of June, he begins to lose interest in the topicality and polemical intent of the narrative, and concentrates instead upon what might be called its poetic possibilities. At this point he creates the character of Rose Maylie, seventeen years old, 'so mild and gentle; so pure and beautiful; that earth seemed not her element'. Rose passes through a severe illness, but then recovers. Here we may see Dickens raising Mary Hogarth from the dead. There are also manifold references in the novel to sleep and to dreams, as if Dickens himself felt the need to retire from the world of cares all around him. There are also invocations of 'a happier existence, long gone by . . .' The death of Mary Hogarth had released all the poetry of his being, and as a result it can be claimed that *Oliver Twist* is the first 'romantic' novel.

Yet of course there are also elements of satire and broad comedy, of pantomime and brutal farce. There is the rancid dialogue of Mrs Sowerberry and the humour of the Artful Dodger. And there is Fagin himself, a character out of melodrama who at the beginning is conceived as a comic creation. In one chapter of the novel Dickens described this conflation of many tones and many styles as equivalent to 'streaky bacon'. It would become his characteristic manner in succeeding novels, where pathos is placed side by side with farce, and where melodrama is the companion of comic high spirits.

By the autumn of 1837 he had completed *The Pickwick Papers*, and consigned Mr Pickwick to the attentions of immortality. In one sense, however, he had been dissatisfied with the novel. It had been conceived as a picaresque adventure, and as a result it had become too episodic. He wished to avoid a similar fate with the adventures of Oliver, and so at this stage he began to fashion the novel according to traditional principles. It was to have a beginning, a middle and an end, all linked one with another. So he asked for the back numbers of *Bentley's Miscellany* in order to reacquaint himself with the parish boy's history. It is not at all clear, however, that he managed to straighten out some of the confusions in the narrative over Oliver's real parentage. At a later date, in fact, he confessed that he had 'a very queer notion' of the novel's plot.

He also began to concentrate more upon the central figures of the story, and lavished much care over the portraiture of Nancy and of Fagin. He saw the characters in front of them. They spoke to him. They were so much a living part of his imagination that he was possessed by them. He revealed that at this time 'Fagin the Jew would never let him rest'. He was, in any case, incapable of ease or repose. Almost immediately after the completion of *The Pickwick Papers* he began work on his third novel, *Nicholas Nickleby*. It was written in tandem with *Oliver Twist*, and a routine of work soon developed. He wrote that month's number of *Oliver Twist* first, and then proceeded to the episode of *Nicholas Nickleby*, which he generally managed to finish just two or three days before its publication. It was an exhausting – and unnerving – arrangement. As he came towards the end of the narrative he worked continually and fluently, 'with his mouth wide open, and his face expressive of the most unmitigated horror'. He killed Nancy, as he put it, and then hammered out the flight of Bill Sikes and the punishment of Fagin. And then it was finished. He had written the final six chapters in three weeks.

Oliver Twist, perhaps more than any other novel, is permanently connected with the name of Charles Dickens. Much of his early life is here revived in symbolic form. That is why it remained one of his own favourites. In the latter part of his career he gave public readings from the narrative, and in particular he dramatised the murder of Nancy by Sikes. He wrote notes to himself in the margins of his reading script – 'Point . . . Shudder . . . Mystery . . . Terror to the End'. It had a powerful effect upon audiences, but it also had strange consequences for himself. He became very ill after the readings, as a result of nervous exhaustion and general debility, and it has been generally assumed that his public performances eventually killed him. That is the most compelling irony of all – that the characters whom he had created in the days of his youth had become an insidious presence in his own life.

Yet now Fagin has entered the company of immortals, together with Bill Sikes and the Artful Dodger, and of course with Oliver Twist. The other great character of the novel, not often mentioned in this connection, is London itself. This is the first novel in which the brooding immensity of the city is first explored, and it is the first novel in which the mysteries of the city are aligned with the vision of childhood and the denunciation of neglect. It is a complete and coherent statement, in which the true genius of Dickens is fully revealed.

William Trevor on

A DANCE TO THE MUSIC OF TIME,

by Anthony Powell

'I was born in London, 21 December, 1905, the winter's solstice . . . feast of the sceptical St Thomas, Cusp of The Centaur and The Goat . . .' So Anthony Powell meticulously records, with further details as to time, day, place, state of health at birth, and christening arrangements. The information has a certain relevance when considered in conjunction with a single aspect at least of the vast twelve-volume novel at the heart of his literary canon, since it may safely be assumed that the work's narrator, Nicholas Jenkins, had a beginning that was very much the same. It may even have been that a startling figure such as the Dr Trelawney witnessed by the fictional child and later described as 'a mage . . . with dark locks flowing to the shoulder, biblical beard, Grecian tunic, thonged sandals' was a source of wonder for the real child also, that neophytes were led across Ludshott Common, near which the Powells lived, that an unusual greeting was heard, and a response given:

> 'The Essence of the All is the Godhead of the True.'
> 'The Vision of Visions heals the Blindness of Sight.'

The rented house by the common – 'an Indian-type bungalow', Stonedene in fact, Stonehurst in fiction – was haunted in both identities. An army officer's household, its domestic organisation in the charge of a quietly efficient army wife, the presence of an only child, was the same also. And the shadowing of the real by the imaginary continued: Eton, Oxford, a career in publishing, the bachelor life of 'a spare man' at débutante dances. There was the writing of a novel and a foray into non-fiction, Powell's interest being John Aubrey and his circle, Jenkins's Robert Burton and *The Anatomy of Melancholy*.

'The less novelists descant on their own works the better,' Powell severely lays down; but even so, he allows that 'autobiographical material produced by a professional novelist is bound to raise speculation as to how much direct experience has found a place in his fiction'. And he affirms that from among his friends, acquaintances, or people hardly known at all, he found models for most of his fictional characters. 'If a character in a novel bears no resemblance whatever to any human being one has ever met – nor could ever meet whatever the circumstances – there is likely to be something wrong.' But change, addition, modification and development must follow the selection of a living person as a suitable case for treatment before a convincing fictional figure emerges, such alterations coming 'not so much from thought on a novelist's part as from the uncontrolled subconscious instinct that gives a "character" life'. It is in this role – the writer as portraitist – that Anthony Powell excels.

His first novel was *Afternoon Men*, published in 1931. A few years earlier there had been Evelyn Waugh's debut as a novelist with *Decline and Fall* and a little later Graham Greene's *The Man Within*. But nobody particularly noticed that this burgeoning of talent was significant, or predicted the future stature of three writers who were destined to become giants of twentieth-century English literature.

Powell followed *Afternoon Men* with *Venusberg*, the brilliant *From a View to a Death, Agents and Patients* and *What's Become of Waring*. None was a disappointment: none is now. But among the less enthusiastic critics it became a literary cliché to refer to the novels of Anthony Powell as being about parties and artists, the implication perhaps being that neither provided a desired seriousness. There was the occasional protest about too much drinking and sex. A single strident voice condemned the people written about as 'useless' without revealing on what grounds this judgement was made. But more generally, the reception was favourable, the promise recognised.

In the first volume of *A Dance to the Music of Time* the promise becomes accomplishment; there is a sense of arrival, of a novelist fully in charge of his material, knowing what he wants to do and how he intends to do it. The confidence required to undertake a work that simple calculation insists will take twenty-five years to complete is considerable. *A Dance to the Music of Time* was begun when Powell was in his mid-forties. He was sixty-nine when he finished it.

The early childhood of Nicholas Jenkins is randomly recalled in a series of reversions in time, the most memorable being the occasion when General Conyers and his wife came to lunch and Billson the parlourmaid appeared naked in the dining-room. A set-piece at school establishes Jenkins's friendship with Stringham and Templer, and the presence in the scheme of things of his ubiquitous Uncle Giles, both factors of some significance later.

> 'Visitors are not really supposed to smoke here.'
>
> 'Oh, aren't they?' said Uncle Giles. He looked very surprised. 'Why not?'
>
> 'Well, if the place smells of smoke, you can't tell if someone else smokes too.'
>
> 'Of course you can't,' said Uncle Giles readily, blowing outward a long jet of smoke. He seemed puzzled.
>
> 'Le Bas might think a boy had been smoking.'
>
> 'Who is Le Bas?'
>
> 'Our housemaster.'

Uncle Giles, forever hovering about the Home Counties now that he was no longer a 'restless soul wandering the vast surfaces of the Earth', had dropped in on his way to Reading. Stringham, whose room it was, was crouched over the fire making toast, at the same time frying sausages. 'You'll have tea with us, won't you?' he invited, and Uncle Giles explained that he had never wanted to form the habit of taking tea. 'Thought I might look you up,' he said when conversation flagged.

How he had managed to find the house if he were ignorant of Le Bas's identity was mysterious: even inexplicable. It was, however, in keeping with the way my uncle conducted his life that he should reach his destination without knowing the name of the goal. He continued to take small puffs at his cigarette.

'I see,' he said . . .

For the rest of tea, Uncle Giles . . . discoursed, not very lucidly, on the possibility of a moratorium in connection with German reparations and the fall of the mark . . . Why he had suddenly turned up in this manner was not yet clear. When tea came to an end he muttered about wanting to discuss family matters, and, after saying goodbye – for my uncle, almost effusively – to Stringham, he followed me along the passage . . .

'. . . And so you always have tea with young Stringham?'

'And another boy called Templer.'

'Where was Templer?' asked Uncle Giles, rather suspiciously . . .

'In London, having his eyes seen to.'

'What is wrong with his eyes?'

'They ache when he works.'

Templer was late when he returned. He explained to Le Bas, drawn to the room by the smell of cigarettes, that the train had been delayed. 'I was with a girl,' he corrected that when Le Bas had gone.

'You devil.'

'I was a devil, I can assure you.'

'I suppose we shall have to hear about it,' said Stringham. 'Don't spare my feelings. Did you hold hands at the cinema? Where did you meet?'

'In the street.'

'Do you mean you picked her up?'

'Yes.'

'Fair or dark?'

'Fair.'

'And how was the introduction effected?'

'She smiled at me.'

'A tart, in other words.'

'I suppose she was, in a kind of way,' said Templer, 'but quite young.'

'You know, Peter, you are just exactly the sort of boy my parents warned me against.'

'I went back to her flat.'

'How did you acquit yourself?'

'It was rather a success; except that the scent she used was absolutely asphyxiating. I was a bit afraid Le Bas might notice it on my clothes.'

'Not after the cigarette smoked by Jenkins's uncle. Was it a well-appointed apartment?'

'I admit the accommodation was a bit on the squalid side,' said Templer . . .

'What an indescribably sordid incident,' said Stringham. 'However, let's hear full details.'

School – nameless, but clearly Eton – also throws up Widmerpool. First encountered hobbling unevenly on the flat heels of spiked running-shoes, he looms out of the dusk and drizzle of a bleak afternoon, returning from the run he voluntarily goes on alone and every day, an imposition possibly undertaken because he believes the discomfort involved should not be shirked. Inexpert at all games, he trains for any that are in season: in winter, solitary running; in summer, on the river, 'breathing heavily, sweat clouding his thick lenses' while he drags his rigger through the water. His hands are small and gnarled, his expression aggrieved. His voice is pitched high; reinforcements on soles and heels cause his boots to squeak incessantly, echoing from distant passages. Once, when new, he wore the wrong kind of overcoat, stories about which are legendary, so much so that any inappropriate garment has come to be called 'a Widmerpool'.

In teasing out the foibles of the human condition, Powell's perceptions are ruthlessly keen. There is a streak of cruelty in the ridiculing of Widmerpool by the sophisticated Templer and in Stringham's wit. But cruelty and disdain do not destroy: almost, it seems, they may perversely nurture success.

Such considerations, and an enduring curiosity about people – their caprices, their motives, their way with love, with marriage, what can be forgiven, what can not – charge the narrative of *A Dance to the Music of Time* as it advances. In London and the country, the Gorings, the Tollands, the Huntercombes, the Walpole-Wilsons, Lady Molly and Ted Jeavons feed off a social life that is as rich as it is closely guarded. Granted access to it, Jenkins feels at home there but contrives to preserve his connections with a more outré world: that of Jimmy Stripling and his racing-cars, of Mrs Erdleigh, occultist, of Quiggin with his cultivated North Country accent. Mr Deacon is an antique dealer and dedicated purveyor of penny leaflets. Barnby is a painter, Moreland a composer, Dicky Umfraville a cad. Gypsy Jones is trouble. Sunny Farebrother is consumed by his own charm. Bob Duport is married to Jean, whom Jenkins loves and will love a little for ever.

In a lengthy novel with a large cast, first-person narration – always a confinement – presents difficulties that require exceptional skill to overcome. The point of view cannot change without recourse to letters, diaries, or secrets confided, often unconvincingly. Rejecting such ploys, Jenkins attacks the problem coolly, adopting a casual, anecdotal style as he encourages Uncle Giles to supply him with intimacies from the past which, in one instance, transform the staid General Conyers into the sharp operator of his heyday, with a flair for 'always knowing the right people', and lively in his pursuit of women. Similarly, Bob Duport, during an evening's drinking at a South Coast seaside resort, is induced to release a flood of reminiscence painful to Jenkins personally but useful to him in his task. Stories heard more generally, their source no longer known, are closely scrutinised for defects, 'veracity measured against picturesque detail' when two or three versions of the same episode are current. This painstaking attention – a wise scepticism when gossip is investigated for any purpose, literary or not – lends a verisimilitude of its own to the finally accepted account, and in this case to Jenkins as chronicler.

His role as such, though, is threatened. With unmannerly abruptness, the comfortable England of public-school mores and big-house families, of leisurely university days and agreeable employment is shattered. War, at a stroke, ends the party. Jenkins is in uniform, chastened by the chapel hymns of Wales, then in bleak Northern Ireland, his companions Williams, W. H. and Williams, I. G., Deafy Morgan and Yanto Breeze. The Tolland sisters are scattered, Ted Jeavons guards London from the roof-tops, Eleanor Walpole-Wilson escapes from the social whirl she hates. The great industrialist Sir Magnus Donners is doing well by doing good, Max Pilgrim doesn't cease to play his piano. Prince Theodoric is still with us, but many whom we've grown fond of aren't.

Nothing, afterwards, is the same again. Widmerpool's wartime triumphs, his humiliations too, have sharpened his appetite for power. The awkward, fumbling boy whom Templer once declared so wet you could shoot snipe off him has shed a little more of his vulnerability, sees a future in politics and is already a serious contender, even before he finishes picking up his loose ends. The war has produced a new breed to which he adapts himself without difficulty, a type exemplified by Odo Stevens – clever, suave, of doubtful antecedents, free of morals, generally dishonourable. He's less colourful than Widmerpool but as untrustworthy; as unflinching in his careless disregard for anything or anyone when the main chance is within reach. Pamela Flitton – beautiful, embittered, possibly mad, her 'unspoken declaration that no man or woman could remain unthreatened by her presence' – is still in ATS uniform when she first appears. And X. Trapnel is noisily on the way with the fruits of his genius, *Camel Ride to the Tomb* and *Dogs Have No Uncles*. Redressing the balance, perhaps, there is the advent of gentle, philosophical Pennistone, his small part in the general rearrangement one of its greatest pleasures.

A Dance to the Music of Time belongs to modern literature, a social comedy that eschews the conventional complexities of plot that so successfully energised the great novels of the Victorians. Its title, taken from Nicolas Poussin's seventeenth-century allegory of Time's perpetual dominance, is constantly a reminder of that delicately elegant artefact. The painting's two infants at play are human; so are the four dancers that Poussin has clothed in his familiar colours – his reds, his yellow, his softly luminous blue – as they evoke the seasons. But the old party who plays the music has been given angel's wings, and unearthly horses hurry Time on in the sky. Such disparate elements in unison do not jar, any more than a repeated reliance on coincidence does in a novel that is essentially an artefact too. Coincidence is magic, Jenkins's friend Moreland asserts, and the authorial voice does not demur. Nor does it deny that there is an allegorical presence in these pages, and mystic undertones. The dottiness of Dr Trelawney's cult, and Mrs Erdleigh's prognostications, are sinister in the end.

Fergal Keane on

WOODBROOK,

by David Thomson

David Thomson's *Woodbrook* is a book to which I return again and again. It has been my constant companion for more than thirty years, and yet comparatively few people, even amongst the erudite and well read, seem to have ever encountered it.

It would be wrong to call *Woodbrook* a 'neglected masterpiece' – the standard literary cliché for books that are deemed 'important' but not widely read. The partisans of *Woodbrook* are passionate and more numerous than you would think. After writing a short piece on Thomson's book for a national newspaper I received several letters from fellow aficionados. I know that writers including the late Brian Moore, the poet Seamus Heaney and Ireland's pre-eminent historian, Professor Roy Foster, are fervent admirers. It is David Thomson's remarkable achievement to have written the greatest Irish memoir of them all. And all of that despite being born in India to Scottish parents!

Thomson did not grow up subject to the atavistic claims of any Irish tradition. He came to Ireland when he was eighteen years of age and wrote as if he had known the country all his life – and from the happy vantage point of one who could be truly objective. When he came to Woodbrook, a substantial but not grand country house in the north-west of Ireland, he was still a student at Oxford. The plan was that he would spend his summer holidays as tutor to the daughters of Major and Mrs Charles Kirkwood – the Charlie and Ivy of the book. But over the years the relationships deepened. He would remain at Woodbrook, as teacher, as friend to the Kirkwoods and as the putative lover of their younger daughter Phoebe, for ten years.

To confine *Woodbrook* to the category of memoir is too narrow. It is a measure of the book's extraordinary range and power that it defies easy categorisation. *Woodbrook* is part love story, social history, coming-of-age narrative and elegy. Above all it is a profound meditation on the experience of loss.

He renders us a vanished world without ever lapsing into sentimentality. Nor does he allow the growing burden of his love for Phoebe to derail the narrative. It is a book in which the elements – personal, historical, aesthetic – seem perfectly balanced. It will also delight any lover of the countryside. If you have never visited the wild landscapes of Counties Sligo, Leitrim and Roscommon, David Thomson's evocation of lakes and mountains will surely draw you there. I often carry the book with me on my journeys far afield. I do so precisely because of Thomson's ability to take me back to the beauty of green drumlins and leaden skies reflected on lake water. With *Woodbrook* I can smell the damp hills, even in the Iraqi desert.

At one point he is describing the landscape around Woodbrook in the middle of a winter snowfall:

> The snow was untouched until we marked it and absolutely silent, the sky the palest possible blue, almost white, the air pellucid, but no living thing to be seen for miles except a herd of bullocks huddled and still against a hedge. When the dogs ran over the hill I did not follow them and suddenly felt that extraordinary sensation of imagining myself the only person in the world.

At the heart of the narrative is the story of David Thomson's love for Phoebe Kirkwood. She is barely adolescent when they first meet, a young woman by the book's end. By the time we reach the tragic conclusion we are sure that Phoebe and Woodbrook represent the same thing in Thomson's memory. They are inseparable and lost to him. A lesser writer would make a sentimental mush out of the story of this love affair, but Thomson writes with such tenderness, with so much respect for the memory of what is gone, that he is incapable of being maudlin. Consider this description of a summer afternoon when he joins Major Kirkwood and Phoebe on a ride through the estate. They stop at a stream and are briefly separated, Thomson moving downstream from Phoebe.

There were no weeds. The dark place, shadowy and overhung, where the water looked almost black and where I would have chosen to drink, was beyond my reach and I put my lips to the bright part near me. Phoebe called. I did not answer, but sentimentally tried to reckon how long the water she had touched would take to reach the washing place, to flow along the stream past the Maxwells' house, along to her house, under the avenue and into the brook. It was probably lost in the big lake already, I thought. I climbed the wall and walked quickly to her.

At the end of the chapter, encapsulating that day at the stream, he writes: 'It was a scene from my childhood as well as hers.' And that is the key to understanding the power with which Thomson writes of love. It is always without guile or pretence. The artfulness is in the restraint and, of course, the memory of innocence.

Arriving at Woodbrook, Thomson finds all of his subjects on the cusp of immense change: Phoebe is maturing into a young woman; her parents are heavily in debt and facing the gradual loss of their estate; and the world beyond the house is about to be convulsed by war. He arrived in Ireland as the Nazis came to power in Germany. Although Ireland remained neutral during the war and Thomson's poor eyesight meant he could not enlist, the 'Emergency', as the wartime era was known in Ireland, presaged deepening economic crisis and further increased the pressure on the Kirkwoods.

I have always resisted the notion that *Woodbrook* belongs to the literature of the 'Big House', the world evoked in the writings of Molly Keane and J. G. Farrell among others. Although I am a fan of both writers, I believe *Woodbrook* to be writing of a different order.

This true story set in the borderlands of the Irish north-west is a tale of universal resonance. Change the placenames and cultural references and the world which David Thomson describes – a world frayed by the impossible demands of change – would be recognisable to the devotees of Chekhov in pre-Revolutionary Russia.

I first read *Woodbrook* as a teenager. It was my mother who handed it to me, with the injunction: 'Read this and you'll learn all you need to know about this country.' She taught in a Protestant school in Cork and had a deep understanding of the descendants of

the old settler community. They did not fit any Anglo-Irish stereo-type. They were not wealthy. Many families had intermarried with Catholics. Yet they fascinated me, these children with their English-sounding names. 'Baylor' and 'Spencer' and 'Hornibrook'. As Irish as me, but also strangely exotic, I thought to myself.

Woodbrook is the closest observation we have of the relation-ship between the Anglo-Irish and the 'locals' or 'natives'. I use in-verted commas with great emphasis because Thomson challenged so powerfully the notion of one class of Irish being less Irish than the other. In Ireland the relationship between landlord and labourer/ tenant had developed over hundreds of years, a bond between conqueror and dispossessed which had begun late, and endured. But there was a personal level on which people interacted, a mutual dependency which had evolved, the stories and even the secrets of each other's lives shared over time, which made the distinction between landlord and peasant more complex than official history allowed. In his depiction of the cruelties inflicted upon the local population during the original plantations of the seventeenth century, the Penal Laws of the eighteenth century, and particularly during the famine of the mid-nineteenth century, David Thomson is clear-eyed and rigorous. He does not shirk from telling us that the land on which the Kirkwoods lived was originally stolen from its Irish owners, that previous generations of Kirkwoods were enthusiastic enemies of Irish dissent and vigorous persecutors of Catholic priests. His account of the depredations of 'Coote of Cootehall' is particularly chilling.

But by the time he arrived in 1932, the Kirkwoods were citizens of a new Irish state. It had been founded just a decade previously amid terrible bloodshed, some of it targeting the big houses of the Anglo-Irish. Many thousands of southern Irish Protestants left for Britain or Northern Ireland during and immediately after the War of Independence. The likes of the Kirkwoods or, much closer to my home, the Protestant families of West Cork or the Blackwater Valley, were publicly characterised by some of the more militant Republicans as alien, not of us. It was also a view held privately by some of their less militant countrymen.

With sympathy for the Kirkwoods and their workers, Thomson rescued me from the danger of straying into that myopic swamp. *Woodbrook* is a crucial antidote to the dangerous notion that the Protestants were somehow less than fully Irish. The Kirkwoods did maintain a house in London. In that sense, I suppose, they kept one foot in England. But you never doubt that their hearts remained firmly ensconced in Ireland. Through the story of the Kirkwoods I was to be taken beyond the enduring clichés about the Anglo-Irish which occasionally seeped into the discourse of my

Irish boyhood: 'They're all a bit mad, you know,' or 'So what if they're on the way out, aren't they half-English anyway?'

It was a confused way of viewing past and present. Official Ireland could acknowledge the role played by descendants of planters in the forging of an Irish national identity, indeed in the forging of the very idea of a modern Irish nation. We eulogised men like Charles Stuart Parnell, the father of the Home Rule movement, and William Butler Yeats, our greatest poet. But they were seen as exceptions, acceptable icons, if you like. We were never encouraged to connect them with the dwindling band of planters' descendants among whom we now lived.

While Thomson was tutoring at Woodbrook, the founding father of the new state, Eamon de Valera, articulated a vision of national independence which sought to put as much distance as possible between Ireland and Britain. To the British and the Northern Irish Protestants the neutrality of the Irish Free State in the Second World War was the most truculent expression of this desire. But it was in his articulation of a new Irish cultural ideal – essentially Gaelic and Catholic, based on small farms and self-sufficiency – that de Valera defined his leadership of the Irish nation.

For the Kirkwoods' labourers, Eamon de Valera held out the hope that they would own land of their own. This was no small thing for the 'men of no property' in whose name the War of Independence had been fought. When the Maxwell brothers, tenants of the Kirkwoods, eventually bought Woodbrook, Thomson, in spite of his great love for the old owners of the house, called it a 'just conclusion'. I believe his greatest gift as a writer is his humanity. He can acknowledge the dilemmas facing all of his characters. He resists the easy rush to judgement.

Much of the old Woodbrook estate is now a golf course. When Thomson went back in 1968 he found a sad decline. The great Anglo-Irish estates were to prove to be as much victims of economic change as they were of political upheaval.

I have re-read *Woodbrook* many times. I always open the book as if I am beginning a journey. And always, always, I am beguiled by its beauty and grateful to David Thomson for his generosity in setting this story to paper.

John Sutherland on

SLAUGHTERHOUSE-FIVE,

by Kurt Vonnegut, Jr

Kurt Vonnegut, as I write, is in his eighties and nearing the end ('so it goes') of a career in writing that took off in the early 1950s. In every general account of his achievement, one novel is acknowledged as his masterpiece: *Slaughterhouse-Five* (1969).

Interestingly, Vonnegut himself does not usually call it a novel. In the introduction (Chapter 1) to *Slaughterhouse-Five*, for example, it is 'my Dresden book'. So, too, in interviews – of which, following the huge success of his Dresden book, Vonnegut has given many.

The book/novel opens with a long prolegomenon, which is wholly autobiographical. There is no fiction in these opening pages and a lot of fact. Names are named.[1] The narrative which follows, we are assured, 'happened, more or less'. Between the more or less, of course, is where fiction usually happens. But Vonnegut seems determined to transgress the usual boundaries. Billy Pilgrim's story is punctuated with regular authorial intrusions and the insistent reminder 'I was there'. In two places Vonnegut actually gives himself a speaking part. As their prison train trundles into Dresden, a hitherto unidentified Vonnegut, peering with his fellow POWs through the boxcar grill, ejaculates 'Oz!' It is a Midwest boy's reaction to the Florence on the Elbe. On another occasion, as the prisoners experience an outbreak of collective diarrhoea, Private Vonnegut is heard complaining that he has excreted everything but his brains.

One could make the case that it is the laziness of literary criticism, or the iron categories of the Dewey Decimal System, which have pigeon-holed *Slaughterhouse-Five* as a novel. But neither could one dispatch it with any confidence to the history shelves. There are too many outrageously fictional elements in its mix. The hero, Billy Pilgrim, a time and intergalactic traveller (or perhaps merely nuts), ends his post-Dresden pilgrimage incarcerated no longer by Nazi Germany, but by aliens from the planet Tralfamadore, some 446,120,000,000,000,000 miles from earth, whither he has been transported by flying saucer. This is not astronomy, but science fiction (in which genre young Vonnegut served his writer's apprenticeship).

Billy's imprisonment in a geodesic dome (a style of domestic architecture much favoured by hippy communes in the 1960s) is made tolerable by furniture from Sears & Roebuck (less favoured by hippies), and the even more luxuriously upholstered, but wholly brainless, starlet, Montana Wildhack, who is also flying-saucered across the vast tracts of space as Billy's 'mate'. They will be earthling specimens in the Tralfamadorian national zoo, kindly treated and profoundly grateful for the dome, the furniture, and each other.

Escapism cannot transport you much farther than 446,120,000, 000,000,000 miles into the welcoming bosom of a pliant Playboy Playmate. None the less, the central historical event around which the novel pivots is real. It, like Vonnegut, 'was there', despite what he and others have seen as a deliberate attempt to write it out of history.

The *donnée* of *Slaughterhouse-Five* is simple. On the night of 13 February 1945, three months before the end of WW2, the author, Kurt Vonnegut, was a POW sheltering in an underground animal slaughterhouse during the devastating fire-bombing of Dresden. He survived. On the night of 13 February 1945, Billy Pilgrim, the hero of *Slaughterhouse-Five*, is a POW in the same shelter as Vonnegut during the devastating fire-bombing of Dresden. He survives.

Vonnegut has published many accounts of his Dresden experience. The following is from an interview in 1974:

> I was present in the greatest massacre in European history, which was the destruction of Dresden by fire-bombing . . . The American and British air forces together killed 135,000 people in two hours. This is a world's record. It's never been done faster, not in the Battle of Britain or Hiroshima. (In order to qualify as a massacre you have to kill *real* fast.) But I was there, and there was no news

about it in the American papers, it was so embarrassing. I was there
. . . The way we survived – we were in the stockyards in the middle
of Dresden . . . Dresden was a highly ornamented city, like Paris.
There were no air-raid shelters, just ordinary cellars, because a raid
was not expected and the war was almost over.

We got through it, the Americans there, because we were quar-
tered in the stockyards where it was wide and open and there was a
meat locker three stories beneath the surface, the only decent shelter in the city. So we went down into the meat locker, and when we
came up again the city was gone and everybody was dead. We
walked for miles before we saw anybody else: all organic things were
consumed.[2]

Vonnegut and his fellow American POWs, exhumed from their
underground coffin, were set to work 'corpse mining' – excavat-
ing bodies for instant cremation. The whole of Dresden was a
slaughterhouse.

It's important, in reading *Slaughterhouse-Five*, to realize that
Billy Pilgrim is not Vonnegut. He was based on a fellow POW
called Joe Crone. Crone was, like Billy, comically mal-coordinated,
a soldier always destined to be the platoon klutz. A fellow-prisoner
with Vonnegut, he let himself starve to death before the fire-storm
and is 'buried somewhere in Dresden, wearing a white paper suit'.[3]
Vonnegut resurrected him. Whatever his inglorious military career,
Crone/Pilgrim's literary pedigree leads back to Dostoevsky's holy
fool, Mishkin, Voltaire's Candide and Wordsworth's Idiot Boy.

But primarily Pilgrim is a fictional vehicle for the ironic portrayal
of Vonnegut's parallel experiences, although the Ilium optometrist
could never have written a Dresden book. Nor could Vonnegut's
alter ego, Kilgore Trout – that archetypal SF writer who, like others
of his craft, has great ideas but can't write worth a damn – have written *Slaughterhouse-Five*.[4] In fact, for two decades after the event, it
was not clear that Kurt Vonnegut could write the book. It was not
for want of trying. When he came home from Dresden in 1945, he
records, 'I started writing about it, and wrote about it, and *wrote
about it*, and WROTE ABOUT IT.'[5] As he recalls, Vonnegut covered
tens of thousands of pages before coming up with his 'thin book'.

Slaughterhouse-Five pivots, maddeningly, around the problem of how to write itself. Vonnegut presents himself to the reader as the magician who declares: 'My next trick is impossible' – and then, somehow, does it. No one gave him a bag of tricks to do it with. It was necessary to invent from scratch the machinery for his particular fictional-therapeutic purpose, devising the 'telegraphic-schizophrenic manner of the tales of Tralfamadore' with its intricate ruptures of the conventional chronologies and linearities of fiction.

Teaching himself how to write *Slaughterhouse-Five* was a years-long and arduous process for Vonnegut. One source of difficulty was the author's ethnicity. He was an American with a name more German than most of the enemy he was commanded to kill.[6] He was not sure, even after training, how to do that killing. In his active service, as a scout in the 106th infantry, he 'imitated various war movies I'd seen'[7] – more effectively, we may be sure, than the chaplain's assistant, Private Pilgrim. Private Vonnegut had no love of the military life. He was never promoted and remained, through life, bitterly contemptuous of officers ('they're all shits').[8] He was, when captured at the Battle of the Bulge, a college dropout and, at the age of 22, if not exactly a child, a *naïf* who had never seen more of the world than his native Indianapolis (Pilgrim hails from Ilium – mock epic for Schenectady, New York, where after the war Vonnegut settled down). While it was going on around him – and sweeping him up in its maelstrom – Vonnegut was no more capable of making sense of war – not even the crazy sense it made to the warlords ('shits') – than the infants sent off to fight in the Children's Crusade in the 12th century. Like Pilgrim, they never reached Jerusalem, but ended up in captivity.

Vonnegut's father (with whom he had a difficult relationship) complained that there were never any villains in his son's fiction. Nor is there any enemy, as such, in *Slaughterhouse-Five*. Germans, his father's people, are the only civilized people in the novel, as their city is more beautiful than anything the US can boast. The most hateful figure is Paul Lazzaro from Philadelphia, an incarnation of evil, who lives his life by the motto 'revenge is sweet'. Billy forgives him – even for his own murder. The most contemptible figures in *Slaughterhouse-Five* are 'Wild Bob', the commander who 'lost' 4,500 men, as casually as Bo Peep lost her sheep, and Bertram Rumfoord, the war historian, for whom Dresden is payback to the Germans for their manifold crimes against humanity.

Another problem for Vonnegut in writing his Dresden book was that the event was so overwhelming that a human brain like his simply refused to process it. Where the memory should have been there was only a blank. It was, apparently, a common experience among those who, like him, could say 'I was there' but could not recall 'what happened'. In his head,

> there was a complete blank where the bombing of Dresden took place, because I don't remember. And I looked up several of my war buddies and they didn't remember, either. They didn't want to talk about it. There was a complete forgetting of what it was like. There were all kinds of information surrounding the event, but as far as my memory bank was concerned, the center had been pulled right out of the story. There was nothing up there to be recovered – or in the heads of my friends either.[9]

After Auschwitz, the philosopher Theodor Adorno declared, poetry was impossible. After Dresden, Vonnegut seems to assert, the novel is wholly irrelevant. Or, at least, the traditional novel. There is a telling episode, late in *Slaughterhouse-Five*, when Billy, adrift in New York, blunders onto a talk show about the future of the novel:

> The master of ceremonies asked people to say what they thought the function of the novel might be in modern society, and one critic said, 'To provide touches of color in rooms with all-white walls.' Another one said, 'To describe blow-jobs artistically.' Another one said, 'To teach wives of junior executives what to buy next and how to act in a French restaurant.'

In other words, no function.

American novelists who had, like Vonnegut, experienced war and – like him – wanted to WRITE about it tended to employ the narrative machinery bequeathed them by such masters of American

realism as Theodore Dreiser and John Dos Passos. This was the mode adopted by Norman Mailer (*The Naked and the Dead*), Irwin Shaw (*The Young Lions*), and James Jones (*From Here to Eternity*). Gung-ho Realism was also the mode preferred by Hollywood.

In his first drafts of *Slaughterhouse-Five* Vonnegut evidently travelled the same route – imitating other war stories as, in battle, he had imitated war movies. In his first visions for the Dresden book (if we believe him) 'I saw it as starring John Wayne and Frank Sinatra.'[10] These 'dirty old men', as Mary O'Hare calls them in Chapter 1, declined to serve their country in WW2, but made millions out of playing war heroes. It was Mary, Vonnegut recalls, who argued him out of doing a conventional blood-and-guts war story.

The way forward from his 'how to tell it' impasse was signposted by Joseph Heller (another veteran), who used for his war novel, *Catch 22*, the modish (for the 1960s) techniques of 'absurdity' and 'black humour'.[11] Heller's novel, which appeared in 1961, conceives war as a madhouse. The hero, Yossarian, can only escape the madness by being himself diagnosed mad. But to arrange that would prove him sane. Catch 22. The blackly comic approach to war was also applied by Terry Southern, in his screenplay for Stanley Kubrick's 1963 film, *Dr Strangelove*.

In his war novel Vonnegut went a stage further, into slapstick and SF schlock. Why, he was asked, did he introduce the Tralfamadorians – inhabitants of the fourth dimension – into a serious novel? Was this not travesty? The science-fiction passages in *Slaughterhouse-Five*, Vonnegut replied,

> are just like the clowns in Shakespeare. When Shakespeare figured the audience had had enough of the heavy stuff, he'd let up a little, bring on a clown or a foolish innkeeper or something like that, before he'd become serious again. And trips to other planets, science fiction of an obviously kidding sort, is equivalent to bringing on the clowns every so often to lighten things up.[12]

The main action in *Slaughterhouse-Five* ends with the Serenity Prayer, the mantra chanted at the end of every AA meeting (it adds a nice tang to the piety that the prayer is pictured, in Vonnegut's illustration, on a medallion between the Wildhack breasts). Wise acceptance is the most humanity can aspire to. The other instruction, coined on his death bed by the founder of AA, Bill Wilson, is even more applicable – 'Keep it simple.'[13] *Slaughterhouse-Five* engages with hugely complex issues. So complex, we deduce, that (like alcoholism) only simplicity can deal with them. The Tralfamadorian injunction, 'Take it moment by moment', is a version of AA's 'One day at a time'; and their whole philosophy – which boils down to concentrate on the good moments – has clear affinities with the AA program. It solves problems – or, as AA meetings like to chant at the conclusion of their meetings, 'It works!'

Vonnegut's turn to simplicity as the solution to his narrative problems is cued by the children's carol which opens the novel and the interrogatory birdsong which frames the story of Billy Pilgrim, '*Poo-tee-weet?*' What is the bird saying? Something very simple and very meaningful, we assume. It is, Vonnegut implies, the only possible response to such horrors as the assassination of Robert Kennedy, who 'was shot two nights ago'. Or Dresden. At its most intense moments, *Slaughterhouse-Five* dissolves into childish drawings, catch phrases, white space (in the use of which Vonnegut is a master), or jokes. The death of the novel's one good man, Edgar Derby (based, Vonnegut says, on something he witnessed), is pure *Alice in Wonderland*.

> The irony is *so* great. A whole city gets burned down, and thousands and thousands of people are killed. And then this one American foot soldier is arrested in the ruins for taking a teapot. And he's given a regular trial, and then he's shot by a firing squad.

There is no dormouse in Edgar's fatal teapot, but the logic of his execution is that of the Queen of Hearts. Off with his head.

Simplicity, as any AA member will tell you, is not easily achieved. It was twenty-five years before Vonnegut could give birth to his 'thin', and deceptively simple, story of Billy Pilgrim's recovery (or psychic flight) from Dresden. Nor, despite the awards that enabled Vonnegut in the mid-1960s to concentrate full time on writing his

Dresden book, was it an easy birth. His marriage was in the process of breaking up. Valencia's disappearance from the plot (death by Cadillac) prefigures the Vonneguts' formal separation in 1971. Their eldest son Mark descended into schizophrenia, from which he recovered to write a book about the experience, *The Eden Express*. In it he gives some insights into the disintegrating household circumstances in which *Slaughterhouse-Five* found its final form.[14]

As his memoir recalls, drugs played a part in Mark Vonnegut's schizophrenic breakdown. There is, throughout *Slaughterhouse-Five*, an implied rationalist explanation that Billy Pilgrim's becoming unstuck in time and his obsession with Tralfamadore is either (1) schizophrenic breakdown, precipitated by post-traumatic stress, or (2) that, like many in the 1960s, he has embarked on some kind of LSD trip. Tralfamadore and Montana Wildhack are his Lucy in the Sky with Diamonds. Vonnegut himself has always been adamant that he, personally, has never used other than prescription drugs. 'I'm not on the dope thing. I don't believe in it,' he said in 1972, while all around him were lighting up and dropping out.[15] None the less, there was enough of the thing around at the time for him to have known all about it. And, sadly, about schizophrenia as well.

The passage of time has confirmed *Slaughterhouse-Five* as one of the great American novels of the twentieth century. It has also revealed how, like a fly trapped in a blob of amber (the Tralfamadorians' favourite analogy), it is very much a novel of its time, the 1960s. Billy's Zen-like passivity and the stoical 'so it goes' mantra reflect a period when dropping out was the preferred response to a screwed-up society. So too does Billy and Montana's final embrace of hippy hedonism in their far-away dome. All that's missing is the body paint and the kaftans. Passages in the novel, such as the famous reverse bombing sequence in Chapter 4, hit home more powerfully when, as in 1969, the country's youth were doing battle in the streets for Peace. Billy's son, Robert, makes amends for his adolescent delinquencies by becoming a Green Beret and serving in Vietnam (a hit at John Wayne, whose grotesque pro-war movie, *The Green Berets*, came out in 1968). Billy, in his gentle way, is unimpressed by his son's metamorphosis.

The sixtieth anniversary of the Dresden fire-bombing was the occasion for serious meditation by the former combatant nations and for reconciliation. It also brought with it some revision of *Slaughterhouse-Five*'s polemic. As he testifies in the novel, and in interviews afterwards, the publication of David Irving's silence-breaking *Apocalypse 1945: The Destruction of Dresden* (1963) was a main stimulus to Vonnegut's getting his own work into its final shape. Although much of Irving's research is, fellow historians testify, still valid, the thrust of his book, and particularly the casualty figures he estimates, have come under sceptical scrutiny. For other reasons (charges of Holocaust denial and neo-Nazi sympathy, notably) Irving was not, forty years on, as respected a source as he was when Vonnegut first came across him.

Estimates in 2005 downscaled the civilian casualties to 35,000 – not the 135,000 which Vonnegut, following Irving, repeatedly quotes (and which Irving still maintains as correct). Thirty-five thousand, of course, is not a figure to which one would attach the word 'mere'. But it undercuts, if one wants to do a Bertram Rumfoord, Vonnegut's equally repeated allegation that Dresden was a worse massacre than Hiroshima. Dresden was very bad, but not the worst.[16]

Vonnegut gave an interview to the BBC's Culture Show, on the occasion of the anniversary in February 2005. Aged 82, he was grizzled but unbowed. He repeated the 135,000 casualty figure. Nor, in his view, were there grounds for optimism. Dresden was history, but Baghdad was now: and the same kind of thing. 'Bush and his gang', he said, don't know how to do war, 'because they've never been there.' Lock them in the basement of the White House, carpet-bomb Washington, and they might do their job better – if they were lucky enough to survive. Nor were the novelists of the day more creditable than the gang in the White House. 'My profession', he said, 'have a lot to answer for.'

It was good to hear him, and good to be reminded how funny, brave, and essentially *good* (in every applicable sense of the word) *Slaughterhouse-Five* was – and is.

Notes

1. Principally those of Bernard O'Hare (Vonnegut's army comrade and closest friend) and Gerhard Müller, the taxi driver who took them round the reconstructed Dresden. Edgar Derby, Paul Lazzaro, 'Wild Bob' – although Vonnegut vouches for their authenticity – were prudently renamed.

2. Vonnegut interviewed by John Casey and Joe David Bellamy in 1974, reprinted in *Conversations with Kurt Vonnegut*, ed. William Rodney Allen (Mississippi, 1988), pp. 162–3.

3. Kurt Vonnegut, *Fates Worse than Death* (New York, 1991), pp. 106–7. Elsewhere, in an interview in 1996, Vonnegut recalls Crone as 'Edward'. Many of the details of Pilgrim/Crone's journey from Belgium, and his comical awkwardness in Dresden, came from another POW, Tom Jones, who was interviewed by Vonnegut when researching his novel.

4. Trout, who first appears in *God Bless You, Mr Rosewater* (1965), is (with members of his family) a presence in many of Vonnegut's novels and has a leading part in *Breakfast of Champions* (1973). Trout and Rosewater overlap, marginally, into the first of the hospital scenes in *Slaughterhouse-Five*. It is assumed that Kilgore Trout (many of whose exotic SF works are described by Vonnegut) was based on the actual writer Theodore Sturgeon. In an extension of the joke, Vonnegut records that Trout died, aged 74, in 1981, and is buried under a tombstone with an inscription from his 209th novel, 'We are healthy only to the extent that our ideas are humane.'

5. *Conversations*, p. 163.

6. Vonnegut was born into a wealthy German-American family. His father was a leading architect in Indianapolis, his mother Edith Lieber Vonnegut was heiress to a brewing family, and highly cultivated. (She committed suicide on Mother's Day, 1944 – one of the recurrent personal tragedies that have marked Vonnegut's life.) The Vonneguts, following the 'Americanization' common in their community with WW1, studiously kept their son away from any German cultural influences. He might as well, Vonnegut ruefully said, have been brought up Tibetan or Bolivian.

7. Vonnegut, 'The Art of Fiction LXIV', 1977, in *Conversations*, p. 171.

8. Vonnegut, interviewed by *Playboy*, 1973, in *Conversations*, p. 96.

9. Ibid., p. 94.

10. Vonnegut, 1977, in *Conversations*, p. 175.

11. The term, which came to be overused in the 1960s and early 1970s, was devised by Bruce Jay Friedman.

12. Vonnegut, 1973, in *Conversations*, p. 94.

13. Vonnegut, resolutely atheist in most matters, admits that AA represents the 'religion' he considers superior to all others. See ibid., p. 78.

14. Vonnegut's ex-wife, Jane Vonnegut (later Yarmolinsky), wrote a memoir, published posthumously, covering the same years, *Angels without Wings* (Boston, 1987).

15. Vonnegut, interviewed by William T. Noble, 1972, in *Conversations*, p. 61.

16. The revised account of the destruction of Dresden, with much contradiction of Irving (provoking counter-contradiction by Irving, on his website), is given by Frederick Taylor in *Dresden: Tuesday, February 13, 1945* (New York, 2004). Vonnegut's latest, and possibly last, thoughts on Dresden are to be found in *A Man Without a Country*, ed. Daniel Simon (London, 2006).

Jonathan Coe on

THE HISTORY OF TOM JONES,

by Henry Fielding

The History of Tom Jones used to have the inviolable status of an English classic. I wonder if that's the case any more. The first warning sign, for me, came in 2002, when a very distinguished panel of novelists from around the world combined to produce a list of the one hundred greatest works of fiction ever written. Their selection, as announced in *The Guardian*, included *Gulliver's Travels* and *The Life and Opinions of Tristram Shandy, Gentleman*, but made no mention of the masterpiece which lies chronologically between them. *Tom Jones* was famously described by Edward Gibbon as 'that exquisite picture of human manners' which 'will outlive the palace of the Escurial'. Has it finally started to fall off the map?

Of Fielding's approximate contemporaries, it now seems to be Laurence Sterne and Samuel Richardson who are most fashionable. Both, I suppose, seem on the surface to have a more modern sensibility – Richardson with his commitment to psychological realism, Sterne with his radical and anarchic deconstruction of the novel's formal possibilities. Richardson has also been claimed by feminist or pro-feminist critics. Fielding's reputation, on the other hand, remains hamstrung by a miscellany of lazy prejudices. When people talk of *Tom Jones*, they like to use words such as 'bawdy' and 'lusty'. I have even seen the novel described, without irony or apology, as 'lad-lit'. There still hangs over Fielding the whiff of embarrassment generated by Thackeray's profoundly misjudged eulogy in *The English Humourists of the Eighteenth Century*, where he wrote of his 'manly play of wit', imagined him late in life speaking 'in his hearty, manly way, his eyes lighting up as it were with their old fire', and concluded: 'Such a brave and gentle heart, such an intrepid

and courageous spirit, I love to recognise in the manly, the English Harry Fielding.' Could anything be more calculated to put off twenty-first-century readers? Unless to remind them, perhaps, that Fielding was also responsible for writing a song called 'The Roast Beef of Old England'. (Which I suppose loses him the vegetarian vote as well.)

Well, it is time, once again, to forget all that nonsense and concentrate on Fielding the novelist, and recognise him as the bold and sophisticated pioneer that he was. It's hard to credit, in fact, that *Tom Jones* stands at the beginning of a novelistic tradition in English, so confidently does it stake out areas of formal possibility which have scarcely been touched upon since. There is the plot, of course, which Coleridge identified as one of the three most brilliant in all literature (the others were *Oedipus Rex* and *The Alchemist*). And there is the humour – so generous, and spontaneous, and knowing – an unstoppable flow forever bubbling out in throwaway comments and lightning character sketches. But above and beyond these things, there is Fielding's ambition to create a 'new species of writing', which he hoped would allow human nature to be explored in its smallest detail while simultaneously painting a larger fresco, a panorama of contemporary British society.

For this purpose, Fielding repeatedly refers to his book as a 'history', and sustains a poker-faced pretence that he is merely a recorder of events that have actually taken place. In some ways this severely restricts his perspective: it means that he can only ever write about the things that have been – supposedly – reported back to him, ruling out any real penetration into psychology. (On one occasion, for instance, telling us that Tom has acted out of 'mere despair', Fielding has to qualify this rare insight into his hero's emotional life with the explanation, 'as he afterwards said'.) But it also enables him to pull off the novel's most ingenious formal trick: it tells a complex, engrossing story while at the same time commenting upon itself reflexively, either in the introductory chapters which preface each of the eighteen books, or in the hundreds of shrewd, jocular asides with which Fielding peppers his narrative.

In a way, what Fielding achieved in *Tom Jones* in 1749, was too original and idiosyncratic to inspire imitations. It was Richardson's

Clarissa, published in 1748–9, that became the template for the English literary novel, with its tendency to sacrifice narrative propulsion in favour of a meticulous probing into characters' interior lives, and its somewhat haughty rejection of humour as a short cut to psychological truth. But lofty critics (and readers) should not mistake Fielding for a chauvinist, or some kind of literary music-hall turn, just because he wrote frankly about the male sexual appetite, and did so with a smile on his face.

Tom Jones, in other words, is much more than a light-hearted romp. It is both the first great English novel and the first great English essay on the art of novel-writing. And the fact that it combines these two seemingly incompatible feats derives partly from technical virtuosity, but mainly from the sheer strength of its narrator's personality: what Henry James called Fielding's 'fine old moralism, fine old humour and fine old style, which somehow really enlarge, make every one and every thing important'. Legions of writers have, over the last two and a half centuries, puzzled over the mysteries implied in that little word, 'somehow'; but nobody has been able to explain exactly how Fielding did it. That, I think, is the real proof of his genius.

Julian Barnes on

THE GOOD SOLDIER,

by Ford Madox Ford

In 1927, *The Good Soldier* was reissued as the first volume of a uniform edition of Ford Madox Ford's works. In a dedicatory letter to Stella Ford, the novelist explained that his 'tale of passion' was a true story heard a decade previously from the character he calls Edward Ashburnham, but that he'd needed to wait until all the originals were dead before he could write it. He claimed it as his best book, and asked, uxoriously, that Stella accept not just this work, but 'the general dedication of the edition'. Like all statements by Ford, and many about him, this needs a dose of annotation and clarification. Thus:

Ford Madox Ford was two-thirds an assumed name. He started life, in Surrey in 1873, as Ford Hermann Hueffer, and published his first books as Ford Hueffer. He inserted the Madox as a tribute to his grandfather, the painter Ford Madox Brown, and subsequent books, including *The Good Soldier* of 1915, were the work of Ford Madox Hueffer. Finally, he changed the Hueffer to Ford in 1919 (two years after the Saxe-Coburg-Gothas had transformed themselves into Windsors). So his time as a goodish soldier in the British army – from a deeply unfit forty-one year old volunteer in 1915 to a shell-shocked invalid in 1917 – was spent fighting the Germans under a German name.

The title of his greatest novel was also changed after birth. He originally called it *The Saddest Story*, but given the state of European affairs in the year it came out, his publisher John Lane thought the title inappropriate. In his dedicatory letter, Ford explains how he was on parade one day when he received a pleading telegram from the publisher, and since the reply was pre-paid, 'I seized the reply-form and wrote in hasty irony: "Dear Lane, Why not *The Good Soldier*?" . . . To my horror six months later the book appeared under that title.' This account is directly – and typically – contradicted by none other than Ford himself, in a letter he wrote to Lane from his home, rather than the parade-ground, in December 1914: 'I make it a principle never to interfere with my publisher, but to take it out in calling him names. Why not call the book "The Roaring Joke"? Or call it anything you like, or perhaps it would be better to call it "A Good Soldier" – that might do. At any rate it is all I can think of.'

Stella Ford may have sounded like Ford's wife – which was certainly his intention – but she was not. She was Stella Bowen, the Australian painter. They met in 1918, and had a daughter in 1920. Ford's only wife, Elsie Martindale, whom he had married in 1894, always refused him a divorce and eventually, in 1939, became his widow. Ford must have been one of the few husbands subject to a court order at the start of his marriage forbidding him from having conjugal relations, and also to a court order at the end of it insisting that he perform them. His emotional life was deeply complicated and overlapping, and made worse for all concerned by his indecisiveness, self-indulgence and economy with the truth. Stella 'Ford' had been preceded by Violet 'Hueffer', the novelist Violet Hunt, with whom Ford seems to have gone through a religious ceremony in Germany; whether he was legally, or only psychologically, a bigamist is unclear.

Nor should Ford's uxoriousness in print be taken as a reliable indicator of the state of his 'marriage' to Stella. By the time of the dedicatory letter, he had been through his seismic affair with Jean Rhys in Paris. This was an event of literary as well as emotional consequence, producing three novels in quick succession – Rhys's *Quartet*, Ford's *When the Wicked Man*, and *Sous les Verrous* by Rhys's Dutch husband Jean Lenglet. The most clear-minded of the quartet was Bowen, whose description of Ford in her autobiography *Drawn from Life* (1941) is both affectionate and (rare in this company) truth-telling. Ford, she writes there, had 'a genius for creating confusion and a nervous horror of having to deal with the results'. She also notes wisely – wisely, at least, for anyone who had any emotional dealings with Ford – that 'Falling out of love is as delicate and important a business, and as necessary to the attainment of wisdom as the reverse experience . . . I think that the exhilaration of falling out of love is not sufficiently extolled.' She realised that the affair with Rhys meant the end; Ford preferred to continue in emotional dreamland.

The best efforts of biographers have been unable to identify the original 'Edward Ashburnham', and, by extension, the other major participants in the novel. Some evidence points to a parallel story Ford had summarised eight years previously in *The Spirit of the People* (1907). But since this is Ford, he could have been fibbing there as well. Any final chance of authentification disappeared in a moment of exquisite biographical frustration. Max Saunders, Ford's fullest biographer to date, interviewed Ford's last companion, Janice Biala, in 1987 – eighty years after the events Ford claimed had really happened. Saunders asked her if she had any idea who the originals in the famous tale of passion had been. She replied that 'Ford once told her the names of the people, but she could no longer remember them.' As for the 'uniform edition', whose 'general dedication' the novelist was offering to 'Stella Ford', it collapsed after only three volumes.

Such annotations, extensive and at times seemingly pedantic, are necessary whenever a critic or biographer – or prefacer – approaches Ford Madox Ford. At the same time, what they throw up – the unreliability of fact, the shiftiness of identity, the vast emotional confusions, the driving power of sex and love, the grand hopes and frequent disappointments – serve as a good introduction to his nature and his work. Ford once said that he had a great contempt for fact, while guaranteeing his accuracy as to impressions. This was a perpetual frustration to those attempting to make their lives alongside him (and those subsequently writing about him), but it was one of the motor forces of his art.

'This is the saddest story I have ever heard.' What could be more simple and declaratory, a statement of such high plangency and enormous claim that the reader assumes it must be not just an impression, or even a powerful opinion, but a 'fact'? Yet it is one of the most misleading first sentences in all fiction. This isn't – it cannot

be – apparent at first reading, though if you were to go back and reread that line after finishing the first chapter, you would instantly see the falsity, instantly feel the floorboard creak beneath your foot on that 'heard'. The narrator, an American called Dowell (he forgets to tell us his Christian name until nearly the end of the novel) has not 'heard' the story at all. It's a story in which he has actively – and passively – participated; been in up to his ears, eyes, neck, heart and guts. We're the ones 'hearing' it; he's the one telling it, despite this initial, hopeless attempt to deflect attention from his own presence and complicity. And if the second verb of the first sentence cannot be trusted, we must be prepared to treat every sentence with the same care and suspicion. We must prowl soft-footed through this text, alive for every board's moan and plaint.

Dowell is an American – except that he comes from Philadelphia, where 'there are more old English families than you would find in any six English counties taken together'. His wife Florence comes from Stamford, Connecticut, where 'they are more old-fashioned than even the inhabitants of Cranford, England, could have been'. The Dowells have been living in continental Europe – 'imprisoned' there by Florence's delicate health – as 'leisured Americans, which is as much as to say that we were un-American'. They meet Edward and Leonora Ashburnham, he on leave from service in India, she 'so extraordinarily the real thing that she seemed too good to be true'. The Ashburnhams are what the English call (or what Dowell thinks the English call) 'quite good people'. Yet they prove to be no more 'good' or 'the real thing' than the Dowells are 'American'. For almost ten years the two couples have known one another, though never in either of their home countries: the Dowells move between Paris, Nice, Bordighera, and in the summer months the German spa town of Nauheim. The Ashburnhams join them there. They take tea and watch the miniature golf, they listen to the Kur orchestra; Dowell does his Swedish exercises while his wife takes the waters. Together the couples dance a social 'minuet', they make a 'four-square coterie', an 'extraordinarily safe castle', they are 'tall ships' on a blue sea, proud and safe. Except – has your foot gone through the floorboards yet? – they are none of these things. They are 'a prison full of screaming hysterics'. But it is also true that they are footing that polite minuet at the same time – for nine years and six weeks before 'four crashing days' end it all.

Dowell (does the name deliberately suggest something wooden?) presents himself as a narrator sitting 'at one side of the fireplace of a country cottage, with a sympathetic soul opposite me'. This is a desperate attempt at social and narrative ordinariness. It is not so much that we don't believe the ploy; more that Dowell doesn't have the skill, or the insight, to reduce his tale to a mere fireside yarn. The storyteller isn't up to the level of his own story; he is a bumbler obliged to convey an intrigue of operatic passion which he himself only partially understands. Identity, geography, psychology, narrative: all are riven, all in flux. Here is the third sentence of the novel: 'My wife and I knew Captain and Mrs Ashburnham as well as it was possible to know anybody, and yet, in another sense, we knew nothing at all about them.' Here is another: 'I don't know; I don't know; was that last remark of hers the remark of a harlot, or is it what every decent woman, county family or not county family, thinks at the bottom of her heart?' And here is another: 'Is all this digression or isn't it digression? Again I don't know.' Dowell's attempts to burble out his saddest story – to make sense of it for himself as well as for us – end, as often as not, in ignorance or a question mark, sometimes both. This is literary impressionism of Jamesian subtlety, yet with a crisper delivery; it is also the most perfectly deployed example of the unreliable narrator. But what it absolutely is not is muddle; all is utterly under the novelist's control. As V. S. Pritchett wrote of Ford, 'Confusion was the mainspring of his art as a novelist. He confused to make clear.'

What to hold onto as the floor shifts and creaks beneath you? I suggest the most weighted, and therefore the most dangerous, words of the opening pages: 'know', 'good', 'heart'. These words repeat, and each time prod us into questioning: what can we know about any emotional situation, what does goodness consist of, and what is really in the hearts of men and women? 'If one doesn't know . . . about the first thing in the world, what does one know and why is one here?' This is to be a novel about the human heart: it says so on the first page. Yet the word is set differently on its first two appearances; once plainly, once between quotes. When is a heart not a heart? Answer: when it's a medical condition, a 'heart'. Edward, as well as Florence, has a condition which requires his presence at Nauheim. You might expect that having a 'heart' would mean that 'matters of the heart' were off limits. But this would be false logic: it is the two with 'hearts' who are indulging their un-quote-marked hearts at Nauheim; while the other two, the pair with technically healthy internal organs, have a different sort of heart trouble – theirs are either cold or killed.

This is one book for which an introduction can do little damage in terms of giving away the plot, because Dowell gives it away himself, even if half-unaware that he is doing so. Everything I have quoted comes from the very beginning of the novel when – as it seems to Dowell – he hasn't even decided on a stratagem for telling his story: 'I don't know how it is best to put this thing down.' Yet he has already revealed, in his prelude, large chunks of the smash that lies ahead: a rushing, contradictory, time-jumping, place-jumping stream of lostness, bafflement, ignorance and horror. It is like coming upon a hysteric who insists that everything is normal and he himself is fine, thank you very much. Dowell goes backwards, forwards, sideways, switching times and tenses. He even comes up with an 'impossible tense', beginning a sentence like this: 'Supposing that you should come upon us sitting together . . .' – as if such a coming-upon were still possible. Yet he has already explained that two of the quartet are dead, and as if suddenly realising this himself, he readjusts, and the sentence resolves itself in a 'possible tense', the past conditional: '. . . you would have said that, as human affairs go, we were an extraordinarily safe castle.' Time and again a seemingly ordinary sentence will have contradicted itself by its end; the conjunction 'And' is as likely to lead to a denial as to a continuation of meaning; there are false abuttings and leaky grammatical joints. This is a novel which proceeds, both at phrase-level and in terms of plot and character, by moments of disorienting readjustment, some sly and secretive, others dazzlingly brazen. Facts yield and deliquesce before impressions; impressions are crushed by subsequent facts. What can we know?

In his 1927 preface, Ford stated that 'I have always been mad about writing' (though given the nature of the novel he is introducing, the words might read equally as 'intensely sane about writing'); and later in his life he described himself as 'an old man mad about writing'. His literary lunacy, devotion to high art, association with the Modernists, rackety personal life, expatriation and over-production – of novels, memoirs, poems, children's books, art monographs, criticism, literary history and travel books – always made him an awkward writer for the general British reader to appreciate. 'It is just that the public *will* not read me', he complained in 1929. Trying to explain it further – to himself, as much as to his correspondent Gerald Bullett – he wrote from Toulon in 1933:

> Why should a London public like my works? My constatations of life have dubious international backgrounds; they contain nothing about British birds' nests, wild-flowers or rock-gardens; they are 'machined' with a Franco-American modernity that must be disagreeable indeed to the inhabitants of, say, Cheltenham. To them, on account of the 'time-shift' and projection instead of description, they must be quite incomprehensible and inexpressibly boring. Between the Middle West and the Eastern sea-board of the United States as well as round the Pantheon where those devices saw the light they are already regarded as *vieux jeu*, accepted as classics which you must know of, and used for Manuals in University English Classes. So I go on writing in the hope that, a hundred and fifty years from today, what I turn out may be used as an alternative study in, say, Durham University. And at any rate I have the comfortable feeling that none of our entrants for the Davis Cup will have been kept off the playing fields of Eton by a reprehensible engrossment in my novels.

Were Ford – a keen tennis fan – to have survived until our day, he would have been unsurprised to hear Tim Henman complacently describe books as 'boring'. But he might be surprised, and pleased, to see that *The Good Soldier* and his other masterpiece *Parade's End* have (more or less) stayed in print. Back in the fifties there was a Vintage paperback of *The Good Soldier* with a statement on the back from fifteen writers and critics claiming it as one of the major novels of the century. I am not sure whether calling a novelist 'undervalued' helps or not. Perhaps it would do more good just to assume and assert Ford's value, and to point to those fellow-writers who have been vocal in his cause, from Graham Greene to William Carlos Williams to Anthony Burgess.

And amongst the living? Well, here are two examples. About ten years ago, while writing about Ford, I ran into one of our better-known literary novelists, whose use of indirection and the bumbling narrator seemed to me to derive absolutely from Ford. I mentioned this (a little more tactfully than I have stated it here), and asked if he had read Ford. Yes, indeed he had. Would he mind if I mentioned this fact in my piece? There was a pause (actually of a couple of days) before the reply: 'Please pretend I haven't read *The Good Soldier*. I'd prefer it that way.'

More recently, I was talking to my friend Ian McEwan, who told me that a few years ago he'd been staying in a house with a well-stocked library. There he found a copy of *The Good Soldier,* which he read and admired greatly. A while later, he wrote *On Chesil Beach,* that brilliant novella in which passion, and Englishness, and misunderstanding, lead to emotional catastrophe. Only after publishing the book did he realise that he had unconsciously given his two main characters the names Edward (as in Ashburnham) and Florence (as in Dowell). He is quite happy for me to pass this on.

So Ford's presence, and subterranean influence, continue. He is not so much a writer's writer (which can suggest hermeticism) as a proper reader's writer. *The Good Soldier* needs The Good Reader. It's true that he isn't yet being taught to students at Durham University, but there are still seventy-five years of the allotted hundred and fifty for them to get up to speed. And after that, we can start working on Cheltenham, Eton College and the nation's tennis-players . . .

BIOGRAPHY

Peter Ackroyd
Peter Ackroyd is a bestselling writer of both fiction and non-fiction who has written biographies of many of London's great cultural figures, including Dickens, Turner, Thomas More and William Blake.

A. S. Byatt
A. S. Byatt is the author of numerous novels, including *Possession*, which was awarded the Booker Prize in 1990. She has also written two novellas, published together as *Angels and Insects*, four collections of shorter works and several works of non-fiction.

Jonathan Coe
Jonathan Coe's novels include *What a Carve Up!* and *The House of Sleep*, which won the Writers' Guild Best Fiction Award in 1997. He also won the Samuel Johnson Prize for his biography *Like a Fiery Elephant: The Story of B. S. Johnson*, in 2005. His latest novel is *The Rain Before It Falls*.

Helen Dunmore
Helen Dunmore is a poet, childrens' novelist and short-story writer who has also published eight novels, including *A Spell of Winter*, which won the Orange Prize, and the bestselling *The Siege*, about the siege of Leningrad.

Roy Foster
In 1991 Roy Foster became the first Carroll Professor of Irish History at the University of Oxford and was elected a Fellow of Hertford College. He has been a Fellow of the British Academy since 1989 and has recently published his acclaimed two-volume biography of W. B. Yeats.

Richard Holmes
Amongst biographer Richard Holmes's first books was *Footsteps: Adventures of a Romantic Biographer*, tracking Stevenson's travels through the Cévennes. He has also written award-winning biographies on Shelley and Coleridge, and has recently introduced The Folio Society edition of Shelley's *Collected Poems*.

Fergal Keane
Fergal Keane is one of the BBC's most distinguished foreign correspondents, winning numerous awards for his coverage. His books include *The Bondage of Fear* and *Season of Blood*, winner of the 1995 Orwell Prize.

Tim Parks

Tim Parks has translated works by several Italian writers, including Alberto Moravia, Italo Calvino and Roberto Calasso, and has twice won the John Florio Prize for translation. His many novels include *Tongues of Flame*, which won a Somerset Maugham Award, and most recently *Cleaver: A Novel*.

Philip Pullman

Philip Pullman is the author of the celebrated trilogy, 'His Dark Materials', the last volume of which, *The Amber Spyglass*, won the Whitbread Book of the Year Award in 2001. His most recent work, *Once Upon a Time in the North*, is a prequel to the 'His Dark Materials' series.

Iain Sinclair

Iain Sinclair is a poet and novelist working in London. The author of *Downriver* (winner of the James Tait Black Memorial Prize and the Encore Award), he is also the editor of the anthology *London: City of Disappearances*.

John Sutherland

John Sutherland is Emeritus Lord Northcliffe Professor of Modern English Literature at University College, London. Author of many books, and articles for *The Guardian*, his most recent works are *How to Read a Novel: a User's Guide*, and a memoir, *The Boy Who Loved Books*.

Colm Tóibín

Colm Tóibín is the author of several novels, including *The Blackwater Lightship*, which was shortlisted for the 1999 Booker Prize, and *The Master*, which was shortlisted for the 2004 Booker Prize. His non-fiction includes *Bad Blood*, *Homage to Barcelona* and *The Sign of the Cross*.

William Trevor

William Trevor has written many novels, including *The Children of Dynmouth* and *Fools of Fortune*, both winners of the Whitbread Fiction Award; the Booker-shortlisted novella *Reading Turgenev*; and *Felicia's Journey*, which won both the Whitbread Book of the Year and the Sunday Express Book of the Year awards.

Frances Wilson

Biographer and critic Frances Wilson is the author of *The Courtesan's Revenge*, *Literary Seductions* and most recently *The Ballad of Dorothy Wordsworth*.